Raising Up Revival Leaders

Online Ministry Training in Mentor Relationships

Henry Reyenga Jr.

Published by Christian Leaders Institute

All rights reserved. No portion of this publication may be reproduced by any means without prior permission from the publisher: Christian Leaders Institute, 614 Fulton Ave. Grand Haven, MI 60449 (616)745-7118

Scripture quotations are from the Holy Bible, New International Version, ©1973, 1978, 1984 International Bible Society. Used by permission of Zondervan Bible Publishers. All rights reserved.

Copyright © 2013 Henry Reyenga

All rights reserved.

ISBN-10: 978-1492301318

ISBN- 1492301310

DEDICATION

TO MY WIFE PAMELA S. REYENGA

Table of Contents

Preface – Page 1

Chapter 1: Identifying Revival Leaders – Sending Called and Trained Christian Leaders – Page 6

Chapter 2: Training Revival Leaders – Take the Distance Out of Distance Learning – Page 37

Chapter 3: Calling Revival Leaders - God Calls Leaders – Page 60

Chapter 4: Approving Revival Leaders: Qualified and Ready – Page 78

Chapter 5: Studying Revival Leaders: Start with a Getting started Class – Page 90

Chapter 6: Training Revival Leaders: Effective Course of Study – Page 101

Chapter 7: Being Mentored Revival Leaders - Everyone Needs mentors – Page 120

Chapter 8: Mentoring Revival Leaders - Everyone is A Mentor – Page 133

Chapter 9: Grouping Revival Leaders – Mentor Centers Locally and Worldwide – Page 144

Conclusion – Page 158

About Author – Page 166

Henry Reyenga Jr.

Make a Donation for Training Revival Leaders:

Information (please print) or visit https://www.christianleadersinstitute.org/donate.html (Tear this out)

Name _____

Address _____

City, ST Zip Code _____

Phone: _____

Email _____

I (we) plan to make this contribution in the form of: ☐cash ☐check ☐credit card ☐other.

Credit card type | Exp. date _____

Credit card number _____

Authorized signature _____

Please make checks, or other gifts payable to: Christian Leaders Institute
614 Fulton Street,
Grand Haven, MI 49417

PREFACE

I wanted to bring fresh focus to the calling to raise up Christian Leaders for a world-wide revival of human hearts turning toward God. Christian Leaders Institute utilizes cost-reducing, cutting-edge online technologies that bring training to called Christian Leaders. The training is beamed into mentor relationships that bring support and opportunities for learning to the called Christian Leader.

Christian Leaders Institute (CLI) is a ministry that provides **free** online ministry training. Over twenty-four advanced ministry training classes are offered.

Because the Internet makes the cost so low, our passion is to keep ministry training free of charge. We believe that Jesus did not charge his disciples, nor did Paul charge Timothy. We want to take every possible barrier away to someone getting the ministry training they need. Our goal is to train 100,000 Revival leaders by 2020.

The Internet can bring ministry training to almost anywhere. Revival is needed everywhere. CLI is training leaders in over 100 countries. A large number of these student will be bi-vocational leaders. A large number of existing pastors with little training are enrolling for necessary ministry training.

Bring Revival In Your Community

Are you called? Read about how Christian Leaders Institute will help you. We can give you tuition-free, high-quality ministry training. This training includes online lectures, quizzes, papers, and other interactions. Classes are designed to be very friendly to local mentors and mentor centers.

Find Revival Leaders

Does your church need revival? Does anyone from your church sense the calling to ministry? Does your church want to start a mentor center to raise up local revival leaders for your church? Students and mentors can meet to discuss classes, recognize course and ministry accomplishments, and support each other in the ministry training journey. In effect a local church can start a Bible School. A church could make this mentor center one of its programs, even going so far as meeting regularly to watch video lectures beamed to the church via the internet.

Covenant Life Church in Grand Haven, Michigan is an example of such a church. It has started a mentor center which encourages a leader training culture. These Covenant Life Leaders study online, get credit, and meet regularly at the building to discuss what they are studying.

This book will get you "online" to the possibilities of ministry training. You will get into the soul of Christian Leaders Institute. Find out more about Bible school, seminary-style, online ministry training at Christian Leaders Institute. I hope there is a place for you to get involved. Steve Mvondo of

Cameroon got involved as a student.

"Hi, my name is Steve Mvondo, 23. I am the last born of 7 children. My mother passed 9 years ago. I live in Douala, Cameroon, Africa

I gave my life to Christ in 2001, through the testimony of one of my elder brothers, who invited me to his church. That day I was blessed by the praise, and I answered positively to the altar call. That day I really felt something different had happened in my life. I was baptized three years later.
My main ministry dream is to be a voice for God in my generation and in my country. A leader of people and a carrier of His love and grace everywhere. I want to become a pastor and a preacher.

A scholarship from Christian Leaders Institute will help me because I believe it is important to be effectively trained and well equipped for the mission. I intend to be used by God. I come from a country where it is not easy to have good training at a price I can possibly afford. A scholarship from Christian Leaders Institute will help me get closer to GOD, and to my purpose!"

CHAPTER 1

IDENTIFYING REVIVAL LEADERS - SENDING CALLED AND TRAINED CHRISTIAN LEADERS

Genesis 4:26b Then began men to call upon the name of the LORD.

Once upon a time, everyone on earth knew God and was with God. The first human man, Adam and the first human woman, Eve were created by God and given life. They lived in a garden where God walked and talked with them. Yet our first parents were given a simple but not easy test. Would they willingly stay with God or would they want to "be like God"? Our parents chose to turn their backs on God and fell into a state of sin.

Adam and Eve died to God. God promised there would be revival to bring humans back to God. Even as Adam and Eve were hearing about the consequences of their sin, (Gen 3), God promised that the human race could be revived back to God. God would make a way for us back to himself.

We read in the Old Testament how revival has come and gone. We read the intensity of Psalm 80:17-19.

> Let your hand rest on the man at your right hand, the

son of man you have raised up for yourself. Then we will not turn away from you; revive us, and we will call on your name. Restore us, O LORD God Almighty; make your face shine upon us, that we may be saved.

What is Revival?

Revival is individual and corporate reconnecting to God in a pronounced way. Individual revival is the restoring of a person's spiritual life. Corporate revival is when groups together experience individual revival to God. After the time of Pentecost, this type of revival is very evangelistic in that the Holy Spirit is poured out in a powerful way to many Christians beyond just a few leaders (Acts 2).

Revival has been experienced throughout human history. Adam and Eve died to God. God promised there would be revival. Abel's soul was revived toward God. God accepted his offering (Genesis 4). The world returned to its path leading far from God, but in the line of Seth, people began to call on the name of the Lord (Genesis 4:26).

Revival leaders of the Old Testament, were people like:

Enoch (Genesis 5:21): Enoch walked closely with God to a point that he was directly transported to heaven; he did not experience death.

Noah (Genesis 6)): Noah was the last righteous man on early earth. But he is counted in the line of revival leaders who walked with God. He preached "righteousness" when few listened. God restarted humanity through Noah and revived faith on the earth.

Abraham (Genesis 12): After the flood, civilization was leaving God again. Abraham walked with God and revival was brought back to the earth and a new nation was formed.

Moses (Exodus 2): Israel was in bondage in Egypt. Revival was needed. God used Moses, a Hebrew who was raised in the household of Egypt's ruler. After murdering an Egyptian man, Moses fled to the desert. At the age of 80, God called him to free his people and reintroduce God to humanity, specifically to the nation of Israel. God was going to use this nation as his stage to bring redemption to the whole world and bring revival to people everywhere.

David (1 Samuel 16): The Spirit of God dwelt strongly in a shepherd boy named David. David eventually became King of Israel. He was a man after God's own heart. He brought revival to God's people Israel. He personally wrote many of the psalms in the Book of Psalms. Even in some of his worst moments he modeled what it is like to walk with God. See Psalm 51.

Daniel (Daniel 1): The nation of Israel fell from being close to God under King David to a people who were just like the nations around them. God used a captured boy named Daniel to bring revival back to God's people. Daniel spoke before wicked Kings of Babylon and Assyria. Through Daniel's influence the nation of Israel was recreated. Soon the Savior of the world would be born in this nation.

The Revival that Grounds Every Revival

In the fullness of time, God sent his own Son to bring humanity back to God. The entirety of the life that Jesus lived, his death and resurrection, and his ascension back to His father is the seed for every revival for until the world ends. After Jesus ascended to heaven, he sent the Holy Spirit to bring revival to God, not just to a nation, but to all people.

Jesus had trained leaders for revival whom he called disciples. They were ordinary fisherman. I have learned that God often chooses lowly unexpected leaders for great revival. Or he brings the high low; once God makes them low, he uses them. Jesus met Saul en route to persecute Christian leaders. On the way to Damascus, Jesus showed up. Paul "fell to the ground and heard a voice say to him, 'Saul, Saul, why do you persecute me?'" (Acts 9:4).

God was creating a new church were humans could be revived to God. God was going to use revival leaders beginning with the disciples and apostles. These revival leaders were going to be used to proclaim the gospel and revive people's hearts back to God.

Throughout the history of the church, God has raised up revival leaders even when it looked like the church had lost the flame. While the early church thrived even under persecution, eventually much corruption entered the church. While multitudes were connected to the institution of the church, many people were not revived toward God.

God brought revival at the time of the Reformation. Martin Luther started the leader revival that spread to millions of people. In the Reformation people were reconnected to the Scriptures. God raised up leaders who were not professionals. Revival leaders increased when doctrine of the priesthood of all believers was stressed. The church revived. People revived toward God.

After the Reformation, God has been raising up revival leaders everywhere in every generation. It is not a secret that institutional churches have been hot on God and cold on God. But revival toward God has happened in every generation through unlikely leaders.

Every Person on Earth Needs Revival

Traditionally, revival is a term that is used to describe the revival of the church in a specific time or location. I will use the word revival in reference to revival back to God. I believe that a "seed" of religion is embedded deeply in every human being. I also believe that our goal is to raise up an army of revival leaders whose passion is to reintroduce them to God, the Creator and Redeemer and to keep people close to God.

For those who are already Christians, we want the spirit of more revival living strongly in them. We want those Christians to lead others in revival. For those who are not Christians, we will preach the gospel and disciple them into a living relationship where their dead spirits will be revived.

The Traditional Characteristics of Revival of the Church

Elmer L. Towns and Douglas Porter wrote a book, <u>The Ten Greatest Revivals Ever: From Pentecost to the Present,</u> that chronicles the many revivals from Pentecost to the present. This is a standard book that is a core textbook in our revival class at CLI. Elmer Towns wrote another book with Neal Anderson called <u>Rivers of Revival.</u>

Another textbook of the Missions and Revival class is <u>Ordinary People, Extraordinary Things</u>, written by Dr. Bruce Ballast. Two out of these three books are standard books in the Missions and Revival course at CLI. All three of these book are great resources for seeing the characteristics of revival since the early church. A study of church history chronicles one revival after another. The Church History course at CLI includes this history from the early church to today.

The Verbs of Revival

As I study about church history and the revivals back to God, I have come up with my top verbal expressions that have characterized revivals: Repenting, evangelizing, worshiping, believing God (Faith), holding firm to scriptural truth, experiencing a deeper indwelling of the Holy Spirit, fighting spiritual warfare, filling by the Holy Spirit, reconciling races, rebirthing to a Kingdom of God focus, praying for revival, and raising up leaders.

The Raising Up Bi-Vocational and Vocational Leaders

I found in studying revivals that the revival of the Reformation really centered on a shift in leadership. The existing church at that time recruited church clergy in a hierarchy which usually did not include lay leaders. The reformers saw that the clergy/lay separation was hurting the health of the church. So, instead of the rare priests knowing the Bible and giving leadership in the faith, everyone is included in this calling.

> The Priesthood of all Believers is a doctrine of the Protestant Christian Church: every individual has direct access to God without ecclesiastical mediation and each individual shares the responsibility of ministering to the other members of the community of believers
>
> (http://www.merriam-webster.com/dictionary/priesthood%20of%20all%20believers)

Essentially the point of the Reformation was that everyone is called to be a leader in the faith and everyone is responsible to make a difference in the world for Christ.

As I think about the list of revival verbs, Christian Leaders Institute is called to raise up leaders. We understand that most of our leaders will be bi-vocational leaders, but we welcome already existing leaders to study with us as well. We want to build a culture of raising up revival leaders that includes the forming of mentor relationships everywhere.

There is a world to reach. I believe that God is calling in a special team of revival leaders, who are mostly bi-vocational leaders, that are called to lead the effort to revive the world toward God.

Christian Leaders Institute Mission

Christian Leaders Institute will beam training via the Internet to raise up called leaders everywhere. Calling is very important. Leaders of revival are called by God.

God has compelled "called" believers from every place on earth to seek advanced ministry training using the Internet at Christian Leaders Institute (CLI). This is only the beginning. God is raising up revival leaders.

For the last few centuries, missionary leaders proclaiming the gospel have reached people in various countries and regions on earth. This has created millions of indigenous Christians everywhere. Out of these indigenous Christians, revival leaders will be raised up.

The indigenous Christian capital is in place where Christian mentors and pastors are able to provide a local context for students that enroll at CLI.

Christian Leaders Institute recruits called leaders out of this indigenous Christian capital. We are looking for revival leaders who will bring revival to the culture where they live. We promise to bring them free ministry training and encourage them to go as far as they can go in getting the training they need to effectively lead in their local communities.

Christian Leaders Institute exists to identify these revival leaders who have the gifts, competencies, temperament and passion to reach people.

Christian Leaders Institute encourages those who possess the Biblical qualifications of being an office bearer, as found in 1 Timothy 3, as those who are actually called into ministry.

Christian Leaders Institute believes that this new wave of called leaders are largely going to be bi-vocational. These leaders will not necessarily be called with the expectation of becoming full-time paid clergy.

Christian Leaders Institute is very aware of reproducible systems and structures that last way beyond our time. A student of CLI will be taught how to have a simple, reproducible walk with God in their personal life, with their family, supported by their church. This walk is to be shared with those who do not have a walk with God. The "Getting Started Class" introduces a reproducible walk as the foundation for being a Christian leader.

Christian Leaders Institute believes that we have the opportunity to bring Biblical academic training that would normally be very expensive to every place the Internet is connected. This training goes beyond content posted on a website; students are trained interactively using methods like quizzes and input from a knowledgeable staff of leaders.

Christian Leaders Institute believes that Internet technology represents an opportunity for supporting, encouraging and becoming involved in a great open door to ministry training.

Example of an Historical Revival

Adoniram Judson was a called revival leader. Adoniram Judson was a difference-maker. Adoniram Judson was the first American missionary, at age 25, who was sent to bring people back to God in Burma in the early part of the nineteenth century. Judson spread Christianity.

Judson had to learn the Burmese language, translate the Bible into Burmese, and translate his person into the customs of this new land. After 6 years, he welcomed his first convert to Christianity. It took 12 years for Judson to welcome 18 converts. He experienced war, imprisonment, and the deaths of his first wife, Ann, second wife, Sarah, and several children. Judson's convictions, bravery, and vision have inspired thousands of missionaries who have left the land of their birth and relocated to proclaim the gospel in a new land.

Thousands of missionaries and their families have been sent to foreign missions, to large cities and remote local villages. Many died en route, and many died on the field proclaiming the gospel, but their labor has been rewarded. In every populated center on earth, converts to Christianity are found and churches have been formed. Despite this progress, there are billions still to be revived back to God everywhere in the world.

There is so much to do, and opportunities to open new doors are at hand. The faithfulness of these missionaries has planted seeds for the next wave of leaders, who are being raised up and sent to do, in our time, a mission work that will change the globe.

These converts form a core of evangelistic capital which is ready to be identified, trained and mobilized to reach deeper into regions of the earth not yet reached back to God.

When Judson arrived in Burma in 1820, there was no Christian culture, no Christian church, no pastor. There was no Christian "capital." Judson and his wife, Ann, were the only Christians in the nation. Judson's calling to evangelize the world was the only "currency" he brought to Burma.

This calling currency has always been used by God to build the kingdom of God. Jesus called the twelve disciples, ordinary men whose calling would change the world. Paul and Barnabas were called, and with that currency the early church began building ministry capital in the Roman empire.

Today in Myanmar, formerly Burma, there are churches and leaders who reach the lost and disciple those in their congregations. The investments made almost two hundred years ago by Judson are now bringing tens of thousands back to God. All over the world there is missionary capital that can be built upon to increase its effectiveness.

At Christian Leaders Institute new called leaders register to begin studies at CLI. Many of them trace their spiritual family tree to the mission movement. This Christian capital exists in most areas of the world.

Our goal at Christian Leaders Institute is to invest into building on the ministry capital that already exists within the local church. We position our training to support the pastors, leaders and mentors of individual churches, and they rise up as leaders to reach people in their local areas. The academic ministry content is effectively delivered to students who stay with their local leaders. This is the type of investment that enhances and builds more Christian culture. Our currency is calling. If a leader is called to serve Christ, we want to make sure that currency is placed into the service of building the kingdom of God.

Who Are The Called Revival Leaders Who Attend Christian Leaders Institute?

Christian Leaders Institute includes students from every continent, representing over 125 countries. The nations with the largest representation include the USA, Ghana, Nigeria, Canada, Uganda, the Philippines, Pakistan, India, South Africa and Kenya. The presence of Christian Leaders Institute is also growing larger in the islands of the world.

Characteristics of Christian Leaders Institute Revival Leaders Taking Classes

1. Indigenous and committed to be that way

    Christian Leaders Institute students are generally very committed to staying in their countries. They sign up because they have access to high-quality ministry training in their local context. They have not been asking if CLI training will help them move to another country. They want to stay and minister where they are placed by the Lord. Take Fikre Fikadu of Ethiopia, for example.

"I live in Ethiopia. I was born in a partially Christian family. And I grew up in church hearing the word of God through Sunday school. When I had been reached at seventeen; my walk with God was completely corrupted by the peer pressure and I was lost in the worst addictions; like hard drinking, cigarettes, gambling and all bad experiences.

"At that time many pastors and my Christian youth friends were trying hard to reach me back to the Lord, but I first rejected them. I was sinking into the deep of worldly things and I have connected all my styles with the technological developments now available here.

"However, I am always marveling at in my life, even in my worst conditions, God would never let me down!

"Radical changes occurred in my life after my Lord God visited me with his merciful eyes. I received grace before him and all men. Today even if there are some challenges in my life; my joy is now in the Lord!

"My major ministry dream is to reach the lost and those who are under the devil's captivity bringing them to the Lord.

"God is good! I hope that as God raised Christian Leaders Institute, so many servants of the Gospel like me will benefit and be used.

"To tell you the truth at this time I could not afford payment for learning. So, CLI is very important for the realization of my childhood dreams by having the chance of acquiring a good knowledge about the Lord and scripture with the help of the Holy Spirit."

2. Generally Poor in Monetary Resources

Christian Leaders Institute students are often poor, but have enough resources and social capital to have received an education and to have access to the Internet. We will even receive phone calls from cell phones in Africa concerning a question. We habitually invite students to donate to Christian Leaders

Institute, and though they do not have large amounts to give, they still give generously. We have received $200-$300 contributions from students in Africa, for instance.

In America, the demographic includes: urban and rural poor who have little else than an Internet connection, disabled leaders, leaders in the Christian Reformed or Reformed Church who know some of the instructors, home-schooled graduates, and a large group of fifty-year-old and above leaders who are sensing a calling into ministry later in life.

3. Bi-vocational Leaders

We have noticed that CLI is supporting those leaders who really want to explore a bi-vocational vision. CLI students generally expect they will be working bi-vocationally in their country of residence. While the allure of an invitation to study in western countries will entice some of the brightest and most academically wired students into western programs, our students will be passed over for these expensive programs and ordinarily will stay in their own country to become pastors, whether they receive quality ministry training or not.

They are hardworking Christians who are called to bi-vocational ministry. Many times these leaders are called to become pastors and teachers. Sometimes these leaders are called to start ministries.

Take, for example, Tony Wetmore of Crestline, California, USA, who is taking the Christian Leaders Training so that he can more effectively start a ministry. Listen to his story.

"My name is Tony, and I live in a small town called Crestline, in California, USA. Within an hour drive is the Los Angeles basin, where millions and millions of people live, most in darkness, many in addiction, in jail, on the streets, and lost, hurting, without hope. I believe my country has become mostly post Christian. I believe it's time to shred the darkness, and turn up the LIGHT!

"I'm a believer and follower of Jesus Christ. I came to the Lord at YMCA camp when I was 12, and participated in youth groups through high school. I fell away from the Lord shortly after graduating, and spent 10 years in the "world." I then reconnected with the Lord, and became born again. I'm married to a wonderful wife for 25+ years, and have 3 incredible children. I have always been a ministry leader in my church - Youth, Homeless, Prison, and Worship Leader to name a few. I am a First Responder/Emergency Medical Technician on a 911 ambulance in Riverside

County, where I am able to pray over, and with, my patients in times of crisis and need.

"My ministry dreams are to become a non-profit 501(c) 3, and create a ministry, Church, and program that serve all of "the least of these" (Matthew 25:31-40). To tell people, lost people, hurting people, abused people, and young people about the love and saving grace that can only come through our Lord and Savior, Jesus Christ. To help make the change from bread and water of this world, to the bread of life, and living water of Jesus Christ!

"A scholarship with CLI will work around my very difficult work schedule, and ministry life, and will give me the much needed ability and knowledge to minister and pastor better, more completely, and more intelligently, to this hurting world."

4. Technologically Savvy

We have noticed that our students are technologically savvy even if they live in the remotest parts of the world. Internet access is more common than sewer lines in some countries. In places like America, the United Kingdom, South Africa, and other western nations, the students who apply, though poorer by the standards of their mainline culture, navigate the web very well and ordinarily know exactly what to do to succeed at CLI. We have also seen that many retired called ministry leaders will actually get their children to explain how to interact better through the technology of the Internet.

When we started offering online classes in 2006, many remote places of the world were not ready for online training. Today, I am at times surprised at how savvy students really are as they understand and make use of the technology. I believe that we have only just begun to see how effectively new Christian leaders can be trained online!

5.   Ordained Pastors lacking respected Ministry Training

There is a large group of CLI applicants that already have been ordained as pastors or church planters. Many of them have been desperately seeking advanced training but are sadly unable to acquire it. In many places in the world, targeted missions money supporting specific mission goals has supplied only certain needs for training, neglecting to meet other important needs of pastors and church leaders.

This is especially true when training leaders for church planting. Large western ministries have invested in helping bi-vocational leaders to plant a church, but these same leaders do not receive training in other areas that western pastors are trained in at seminary. This causes sustainability issues. It is difficult for the development of a full sphere of Christian culture to be cultivated by these leaders.

These leaders have expressed great disappointment over this situation. They communicate that they feel like second-class pastors because the pastors that do receive the western-supported training are considered more qualified and are given more opportunities, not based on the quality of their walk, their ministry effectiveness, or the specifics of their calling and gifts, but simply on their connection to the western-prescribed training path.

The training opportunities that are funded for these leaders are dumbed down or specialized in such a way that it leaves most indigenous pastors lacking the standing they need to really thrive in their country.

Christian Leaders Institute is committed to giving a ministry training that allows graduates the standing to thrive even in relationship to pastors that have attended traditional residential seminaries.

6. Educated

Christian Leaders Institute students are smart. They know how to communicate. They are often bi-lingual, with English being their second language. Large percentages of them would thrive at residential seminaries, but would never have the opportunity to enroll, because they are too poor or their situation in life prohibited residential ministry training.

7. Respected in their Culture

In countries that are not hostile to Christianity, our students are highly respected. Even clergy in their countries who had residential training from western sources are mentoring students from CLI and encouraging them to get their diplomas.

8. Generally Older and Already Tested

Four out of every five students are 35 and older. Because of where they are in life, these older students are not in a position to go to a residential program, and distance-learning programs are difficult and still too expensive. This group of leaders is generally not going to move anywhere.

9. Often in Countries where it is difficult to lead in Christianity

CLI can offer training to places that Christianity is having difficulty penetrating. We have trained students in Pakistan, Saudi Arabia, and Libya, and these are just a few places our students get the training to create Christian culture, despite the resistance of their country. Sadly, we suspect that some of our students have been persecuted for their Christian witness. In light of this, we do everything we can to keep their identities secret.

10. Very Remote Places

We are training students in remote islands where western missions money would never be able to support quality ministry training. These students are being trained in places like Samoa, Martinique and St. Kitts.

11. Disabled Students

We are training students who have been disabled and are called. Christian Leaders Institute has taken the training to their homes where they can access this training in an environment that provides for their specific challenges. I have been moved to praise God when I hear some of the stories of those who face such challenges.

What about digital chaplains? Chaplains who can "chat" with people who need ministry? Christian Leaders Institute bought the domain names, "chatplain.com -.org. Notice the spelling, "chatplain" similar to "chaplain." I would love to start a ministry where we mobilize Christian leaders to "chat" and minister to people in need interacting on the Internet. It is exciting to consider all the different ways that God can use his people to minister to others.

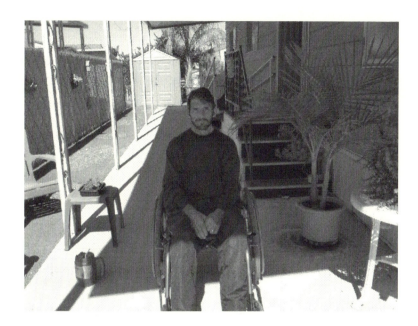

Mark writes,

"Hello, my name is Mark Ziegelhoefer. I'm 53yrs old and blessed to be born into an Orthodox Jewish family. Temporarily, I'm paraplegic due to a spinal injury, which is drug-related, consequences of my past sins. Also, I have been diagnosed with Hepatitis C, drug-related as well.

"Now, I am awaiting the Lord's perfect timing for my physical healing. In August 2001, the Lord brought me a beautiful woman, who is now my wife, Kerrie. She has been a Christian since her childhood. In 2004, I accepted Jesus Christ as my Lord and Savior. Since I have past experience of 32yrs in drug abuse, my dream is to help others that are still struggling with chemical addictions. Knowing Jesus was the only way that I was able to overcome drugs, I want to help lead others to Jesus. I tried all the other ways to freedom from drugs and I know for a fact that Jesus is the only way."

12. Immigrants

Many students have immigrated to new countries looking for new opportunities; countries like Great Britain, Spain and Canada. These students come with fresh enthusiasm combining love for their new country with a passion to share Christ. Take Rosette Singson, who immigrated to Canada.

"I live in Alberta, Canada - our Promised Land. For the past few years that I've been here, I noticed that every single moment of the day, lots and lots of people need Christ in order to cope with life's challenges. Because of the lies and darkness that the enemy is inflicting to every human being, I felt the desire to do something for Christ's Kingdom.

"It is in the midst of my troubles, my pain and suffering that I encountered Christ. So, I thought, it is just right to share Him to others whose only hope is Christ. It is my dream to see the lost restored and find the Way, The Truth and The Life - Jesus - through my ministry.

"I continue to believe for God's guidance and intervention towards the ministry and the calling He has for me. He is the Alpha and the Omega."

13. Very willing to contribute

Many students are doing what they can to donate back to Christian Leaders Institute. We are praying that as our students graduate and plant and pastor churches, they will be able to contribute more and become mentors for future students, making better and better training available to church leaders.

A student emailed this comment on August 31, 2013 in response to a student fundraising appeal. He donated $720 US Dollars,

"I would like to first thank you for following the Lord's calling on your heart to create CLI. I have been studying at CLI only since the end of June, but it has already blessed me tremendously in my walk with Christ. I am also blessed by having the opportunity to donate to this great mission and help my brothers and sisters around the world who otherwise could not afford such high-quality teaching. I thank you and the entire CLI staff for allowing God to use you in this ministry."

Is this "Free" Opportunity a Good Idea?

Christian Leaders Institute offers free tuition. Why? Many have asked this. Some have wondered whether it will be valued if it is free. Some have said that we have so many students, let them pay for it themselves. Others have said that you will never be a sustainable ministry unless the student pays for the education and outside funding is not needed.

I have reflected on this a long time. I have prayed about this much. I have researched business models and consulted with traditional institutions.

I read the Bible and do not see a charge for training people to be leaders. I just can't see that Peter and John gave tuition to Jesus in the form of currency. The only currency that was given was the currency of calling. "Come follow me." That was it! When they followed Jesus, He trained them to be the first leaders in the new church. Jesus had his supporters who paid for the training culture. First there was God, the Father and the power of the God-head. When they needed to pay taxes, they had the option of getting currency out of a fish. I love how Jesus funded a tax they had to pay, "But so that we may not offend them, go to the lake and throw out your line. Take the first fish you catch; open its mouth and you will find a four-drachma coin. Take it and give it to them for my tax and yours" (Matthew 17:27).

Jesus also had financial supporters such as Joseph of Arimathea. We don't know whether he contributed to Jesus while Jesus was training his disciples, but we do know that his funding of Jesus's ministry at his death illustrated the faithful involvement of a truly "board level" supporter.

"Now there was a man named Joseph, a member of the Council, a good and upright man, who had not consented to their decision and action. He came from the Judean town of Arimathea and he was waiting for the kingdom of God. Going to Pilate, he asked for Jesus' body. Then he took it down, wrapped it in linen cloth and placed it in a tomb cut in the rock, one in which no one had yet been laid" (Luke 23:50-53).

After Pentecost, we see the out-pouring of support for the early church by people like Barnabas. "Joseph, a Levite from Cyprus, whom the apostles called Barnabas (which means Son of Encouragement), sold a field he owned and brought the money and put it at the apostles' feet" (Acts 4:36-37). Barnabas was an ideal "board level" supporter and sponsor. He not only contributed to the funding of the church, he also helped expand the number of leaders by sponsoring Paul and connecting him to the apostles. Barnabas had credibility with the apostles. He was an encourager, supporter and networker for the development of leadership capital.

It appears that Barnabas offered his mentorship of Paul free of charge. Paul supported himself as a tentmaker while he was being trained and made ready. Barnabas was so committed to ministry training that it even created a disagreement between himself and Paul. Barnabas, being Barnabas, wanted to give a younger leader, Mark, a second opportunity. Paul did not want to drag the mission march down with someone that might not work out. Barnabas and Paul separated. Later Mark and Paul worked closely together. Mark hung out with Peter, who helped him write the gospel of Mark.

Paul went on to do ministry training with lots of leaders like Titus and Timothy. Most of these early leader recruits were bi-vocational and we have good reason to believe that their ministry training was free.

I believe that there are leaders like Joseph of Arimathea and Barnabas who provide the leadership capital for the development of Christian leaders.

No One Missed

Christian Leaders Institute desires to make ministry training tuition-free so no viable, called revival leaders are missed. This mission is mobilizing a large number of trained ministry leaders. As you read this book, you get more of an idea of why it is possible to be ambitiously training thousands of revival leaders. The leaders are out there waiting to be trained.

"It was He who gave some to be apostles, some to be prophets, some to be evangelists, and some to be pastors and teachers, to prepare God's people for works of service, so that the body of Christ may be built up" (Ephesians 4: 11-12).

The Profile of the Intrinsically Motivated

Finally, free tuition is a test. Those that do well with free tuition are motivated internally at a deeper level. Charging tuition does bring a form of ownership, to the point that the ministry training is given a monetary value which helps in creating a force to complete the studies. When something labor-intensive like ministry training is free, the prime force the student has is his God-motivated call into the ministry. Students lose nothing if they stop their training. They gain greatly if they finish their training.

The profiles of the students that complete classes at Christian Leaders Institute are profiles of "called" leaders who complete goals and challenges because they need to and want to!

CHAPTER 2

TRAINING REVIVAL LEADERS -TAKE THE DISTANCE OUT OF DISTANCE LEARNING

<u>1 Corinthians 9:22-23</u> To the weak I became weak, to win the weak. I have become all things to all men so that by all possible means I might save some. I do all this for the sake of the gospel, that I may share in its blessings.

What would happen if a person I'll call Jason invented an energy conversion box? This invention could convert air into electricity and is scalable. The smallest boxes replace batteries of all sizes. Larger boxes energize cars, small generators and wells in remote areas. Big convertor boxes could run industrial applications and power plants. On top of this, the design is simple, and maintenance costs are very low. Jason's concept is simple to the point that it could be copied easily and would supply a productive resource that would enhance the lives of billions of people.

Just imagine the results! New wells could be dug and a conversion box generator would run a little motor that pumped fresh water to those who needed it. Laptops would never have to be recharged. Cars would no longer need gas and carbon pollution could be seriously reduced. Trains never need to burn stinky diesel fuel, and goods and services could be brought to the market for a fraction of the cost. Propeller airplanes would make a comeback and these planes would never run out of fuel. The effects of this discovery would revolutionize our way of life quickly.

But wait! Not everyone would be excited about this new technology. The production of energy is an immense and lucrative business, and this invention would render fossil fuel companies and nuclear power obsolete! Where teams of scientists and specially trained hazard workers are required for nuclear energy, the simplistic energy box can be manufactured by a simple assembly line! Suddenly there would be thousands of people whose years of training for lucrative jobs were now wasted, and many of them will still have large debts from their extensive education!

Then there are people who would resent this technology for other reasons. Forget carbon emissions and pollution, a "car" is something unique and familiar! They would never consider getting an "electric" car because a "real" car is made up of much more than metal and motor. What really "makes" a car are things like the sound of the gas engine and the feel of the shifter against the hand.

Then, of course, governments would fight to control this new technology. Combat vehicles that would usually consume immense amounts of fuel could now be operated solely off of an unlimited clean power supply! Field electrical equipment would no longer require expensive and bulky generators with specially trained operators to implement them. Everything could be operated from this small, inexpensive energy box.

Now imagine that Jason decided he would give this technology away before anyone tried to own it and make money on it. He legally made it public domain and sent all the secrets for its development and design to everyone. He did not benefit financially from it, nor did he care about financial reward. It was his gift to humanity, period.

Over time, every industry, government, and people group would somehow incorporate this invention. Some companies would keep their old technology and use only small contributions of the convertor box design; other companies would redesign their entire product lines around this resource. Some companies would go out of business and new companies would form. The world would be a different place.

The Internet is like the "Conversion Box"

The Internet has changed the world radically when it comes to the exchange of information and resources. While the invention of the computer was revolutionary, the Internet has brought a new form of connectivity that has changed how everything works, from relationships to exchange of information. Many authors and commentators have chronicled the massive changes that have taken place.

Type into the Google search box, "How the Internet has changed the world," to get thousands of hits from news articles to academic papers. Many saw the significance of the Internet, but many did not see it as a threat to how they operated. The changes that have and will occur because of the Internet are so many and varied that almost no one argues that they can even be overstated.

For instance, the Internet has changed our behaviors and practices in many ways. Here are a few examples:

- How someone buys almost anything, including airline tickets, travel arrangements, books and e-books, golf clubs and poodles.

- How someone communicates with other people. First there was e-mail. Now social networking sites such as Facebook and Google Plus have connected over 1.5 billion people. These social networking sites are replacing phone directories. Someone is more likely to connect via Facebook then actually make a physical phone call.

- How someone researches information. Google, Yahoo and Bing are really just digital libraries. While there is misinformation on the Internet, a discerning researcher would rather have a library brought into his/her own home or workplace to research anything from where to eat to what poodle to buy using the Internet.

- How politicians are elected. Blogs and Vlogs, social media, and other ways of using the Internet are now often a factor in who gets elected.

- How likeminded people find each other. Likeminded researchers can now connect instantly from different places of the world to compare notes as they solve problems together. Those interested in eating organic foods can chat, blog, message and build organic food culture together.

- How knowledge and teachings are transmitted to individuals. The development of Wikipedia and TEDs University has become a resource that many use as they seek knowledge and training about a whole host of topics. Some schools and universities have jumped on the bandwagon, offering distance-learning classes that allow students to do classes online and get credit at the academic institution.

The Impact On Training Revival Leaders

The Internet cannot be ignored. It changes the way humans learn. It changes the way information is transmitted. It provides a tool for interaction that can be used effectively in providing accountability and interaction. Open-source programs like Moodle.org allow schools and institutions to interact in a world-class way with students. The Internet's role in equipping called revival leaders for ministry will continue to increase.

Christian Leaders Institute has a meaningful interactive relationship with thousands of ministry students.

Student Profiles

When students are making their way through the getting started class, they receive a student profile which places them on our roster.

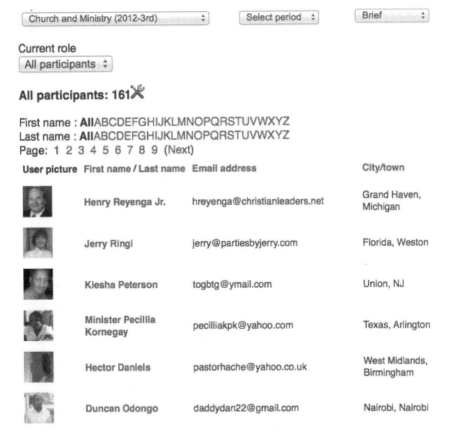

Online Lectures

The professors prepare and place lectures in the digital syllabus. This lecture can be viewed over and over again.

Every time students view lectures, those viewings are recorded in student viewing logs. In other words, the professors know which students are watching the lectures.

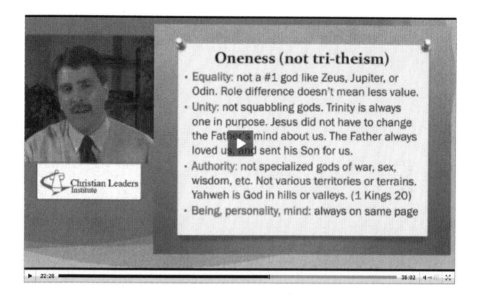

Quizzes and Examinations

Christian Leaders Institute professors assign students quizzes and examinations of their learning. The quiz and examination grades are automatically recorded and saved. At the end of the semester, the quiz results are automatically tallied and a grade for each class is assigned. There are technological safeguards that make it very hard for students to cheat. While this all sounds complicated, the fact is that the quizzes and examinations and the professors' involvement with the students work is presented to both students and professors with an easy interface.

Question 7
Not yet answered
Marked out of 1
Flag question
Edit question

Which of the following is NOT true of God's secret will?

Select one:
- a. God's secret will is identical in every way to his revealed will.
- b. God's secret will hides the good news from some and reveals it to others.
- c. God's secret will means that he plans many things without revealing them to believers.
- d. God's secret will decrees everything that will happen, even bad things.

Question 8
Not yet answered
Marked out of 1
Flag question
Edit question

A theophany is _____.

Select one:
- a. A chorus of humans praising God for his mercy.
- b. Another word for God's truthfulness.
- c. God taking a visible form to show himself to people.
- d. God's infinite majesty that no one can see and remain alive.
- e. A chorus of angels praising God for his beauty.

Question 9
Not yet answered
Marked out of 1

The video "Seeing the Lord of Hosts" highlights four things in Isaiah's vision of God. Which of the following is NOT one of those things?

Students Submit Papers

Students watch lectures, take quizzes and tests, but also participate in submitting papers. We ask students to submit their sermons for evaluation in their mentor relationships. There are so many features that I could tell you about, but I do not want to make this book into a technology manual for Internet ministry training.

The technology is so effective and inexpensive that Christian Leaders Institute can offer an online ministry training education for a fraction of what it costs traditional seminaries to provide the training. It is so efficient that Christian Leaders Institute can make a high impact with a smaller budget than traditional ministry training organizations.

The Internet allows Christian Leaders Institute to return to practices that are very ancient in the identifying and training of a Christian leader ready for bringing revival. To get a fuller understanding of why something so cutting edge as the Internet can help us return to something so ancient, let's look at the ancient practices of ministry training.

Ancient Biblical Practices of Ministry Training

In the Old Testament, revival prophets were trained at the school of the prophets. A snap shot into this culture is easily seen with the life, ministry and work of Elijah and Elisha. In those days, three thousand years ago, there were seminaries for various religions. There were schools for Baal worship where Baal leaders were raised up to promote the Baal religion. In Israel in 1000 BC, the king and queen of Israel, Ahab and Jezebel, were big supporters of the Baal religion. In fact, they were making the national religion of Israel to be the worshiping of Jezebel's god, the god of Ekron.

The minority religion was the religion of Yahweh. Elijah was the only prophet left out of 7000 people that did not worship Baal. Elijah began a school of the prophets by calling Elisha and calling him into the service of the Lord. By the time of Elijah's death, Elisha was ready to take the mantle. Elisha expanded this school even more.

How were the prophets trained? Basically, they just spent time being mentored by their leaders until they were ready to be prophets themselves. This was clearly a mentor model, where local mentorship raised up prophets. The leading prophet modeled the way of the Lord and taught it to the called, yet-to-be trained, new prophet.

In the New Testament, Jesus set up a school of the prophets, whom he called disciples. The Son of God called ordinary people, usually from the working class, fishermen and tax collectors, to be future revival leaders. We see in his ministry that Jesus knew the Old Testament and spent his time sharing and teaching insights about the kingdom of God that would be ushered in when Jesus himself would die, rise from the dead, and ascend on high.

Jesus also promoted the mentor model, where a long-term relationship accompanied by teaching prepared the disciples to be the prophets of the early church. The wisdom of this model was questioned by the religious leaders of Jesus' day, but the power and effectiveness cannot be denied. Consider how the leaders of the Jewish religion characterized Peter and John after Jesus had ascended to be with God. We find that, "When they (the religious leaders) saw the courage of Peter and John and realized that they were unschooled, ordinary men, they were astonished and they took note that these men had been with Jesus." (Acts 4:13).

The mentor model was the model that drove ministry training in the Old and New Testament. When the apostle Paul was chosen as God's instrument to spread the church to the Gentiles, he too worked with the mindset of a mentor. This model included spending time with the newly called future prophets. A great example of this is his work with Timothy, whom he called his son. First and Second Timothy are examples of mentor "content" that even forms part of Scripture.

By the time the apostles had passed away, their teachings and the teachings of Christ were written down for the Christian leaders. They in turn passed on the knowledge content of the faith to newly called leaders. A revival witness passed down generation after generation. The mentorship model was firmly the dominant model for the identifying, training and mobilizing of future leaders, or, as they were then called, pastors. Pastor training was clearly a mentoring operation that included communicating the content of the faith.

This discipleship model yielded elders, deacons and pastors who populated the leader teams of the early church. They were used by God to spread the gospel, and the church spread quickly. This mentor model gradually changed to a more corporate model for the training of leaders.

Within five hundred years, the church organization developed and resembled the cultural organizations of the time. For example, the monastic movement developed, cloistering leaders away from the very culture they were called to reach. These organizational developments themselves did not stop the church from proclaiming Christ as Lord, but the church drifted and its focus became perpetuating its organization as much as a walk with God in Christ.

The Development of Traditional Seminaries

The church continued to drift away from a Christ-centered curriculum until, by the time of the Reformation, very little scripture was actually used to instruct the prophets. Instead, church traditions and practices, as they developed, formed the core curriculum that was communicated to leaders of the church.

The church of God stagnated. She was no longer the vibrant, powerful body of believers that Jesus had instituted. But, as always, God remained in control. He raised up reformers and the technology of the printing press, allowing the original words that taught Timothy to be the core curriculum for future church leaders. This changed the entire church philosophy. Once the actual words of the Old and New Testament formed the content of the faith that was to be passed down, a major reformation occurred.

This scriptural content blossomed anew in the Church. Catechisms like the Westminster Confession and the Heidelberg Catechism brought to the center the scripture as the only rule for life and teaching. The early monastic (seminary) model was continued as in the Catholic Church, but the content was now founded on the Scriptures and the confessions of faith.

The word seminary is from the Latin, "seminarium," which means "seed bed". Roman Catholics started calling their ministry training institutions "seminaries" at the time of the counter-reformation. At these Roman Catholic seminaries personal discipline and philosophy were central.

Comparisons of Ministry Training Models

If we compare the seminary model with the discipleship model, we have to be very careful not to talk about the advantages of one model while criticizing the disadvantages of the other model. We have seen much blessing and challenge from both models of ministry training. Let's compare them.

The Discipleship Model Strengths:

> Local and contextual: New pastors and church planters are mentored locally, and this local connection makes them more effective as they minister to the specific people group they are involved with.
>
> Personal Endorsements: The mentoring leaders are usually familiar with the discipleship struggles their mentees encounter.
>
> Cost-Effective: The ministry overhead of classrooms and professors is not needed.

Ministry Opportunities: Effective mentoring pastors provide opportunities for ministry involvement.

New pastors do not have to relocate or incur great expenses; the acceptance of the calling is the focus. This is friendlier to the families of the called leaders.

More leaders can be cultivated for the service of Christ.

This model is more conducive for the development of bi-vocational leaders. Leaders do not accumulate debt and do not need higher salaries to support their serving in ministry.

The Discipleship Model Weaknesses:

Varied Mentors: Many pastors are not that skilled at transferring knowledge and insights for ministry training.

Local Situation Dramas: Sometimes those who are called into ministry threaten the ministry pastors or mentors.

Accreditation: If someone wants to get an advanced degree, this model does not conform to that desire.

Denominations often do not have a good referral system for this model and many times consider their ministry candidates to be less qualified because of their perceived lack of academic training.

The Traditional Seminary Model Strengths:

Accreditation: Many seminaries offer accreditation that allows students to move on toward advanced degrees.

Connections: Many seminaries have connections in denominations that allow them to move around to existing churches and even receive funding for the planting of new churches. Many times these seminaries have connections for ordination within the denomination.

Objective Tests: When leaders leave their local context they are tested personally and this test often forces them to trust God more.

Accountable Academic Training: The paid staff of seminaries specifically holds their students to academic standards that assure academic competency.

The Traditional Seminary Model Weaknesses:

Eliminates Some Called Leaders: Seminaries tend to focus on academics to the point that many called leaders will not succeed at these accredited institutions.

Costly: Most seminary tracks for ministry training are very costly from many perspectives. Tuition, moving, books and many more expenses put people's lives on hold for four or five years.

Not Bi-vocational Friendly: Seminaries tend to not serve the needs of leaders who are called later in life and seek to keep their daily work.

Christian Leaders Institute Approach

The tools of the Internet offer, for some, exciting options that connect the strengths of both models and minimize some weaknesses. There will never be a completely perfect model for ministry training, but Christian Leaders Institute will try to make it possible for every called leader to do well in ministry.

Born Out of Wall Hits

When Christian Leaders Institute was formed, we wanted to mobilize called leaders into ministry. We began by using the discipleship model. We had discovered this model with others in the last decade of the 20th century. We were working this model for many years and hit the walls of the weaknesses of this type of training while continuing to enjoy the strengths of the discipleship model.

At around 2003, it become apparent to me, at Christian Leaders Institute, that some of the weaknesses of the discipleship model needed to be addressed so as to equip more sustainable leaders. Many times I encountered leaders who were so excited about their calling. Many wanted to serve as bi-vocational leaders. But many struggled because they did not have the knowledge and insights needed for long-term confidence and sustainability in the ministry.

I was praying and looking for a way to bring accessible opportunity for training to called leaders. At the same time, advancements in Internet technology were making it possible to put classes on the Internet that could be accessed efficiently and inexpensively.

I started taking technology classes at the local community college. Through the generous donations of a few leaders and foundations, I hired a technology specialist from the University of Chicago, named Jerry Lorenz. Christian Leaders Institute offered online classes in 2006 with six students signed up for training. Most of the classes were just guided self-study, but we found them to be effective in training bi-vocational leaders.

In 2008, I invited Dr. David Feddes to join CLI as the first provost. Dr. Feddes had served as the English radio minister for the Back to God Hour for 14 years and had just completed his Doctorate in Cultural studies from Trinity University in Deerfield, IL. Dr. Feddes had also worked with me in planting a bi-vocational church in Monee, IL.

In 2012, I became full-time in leading Christian Leaders Institute to effectively reproduce leaders.

The Christian Leaders Institute Approach

Christian Leaders Institute seeks to combine the benefits of both the discipleship model and the seminary model for ministry training. The goal is to mobilize as many effective and sustainable Christian leaders as possible for ministry. The revolutionary impact of the Internet allows us to venture into seeking to bring the best of both approaches.

The ministry training approach of Christian Leaders Institute seeks to do the following:

1. Promote Local Mentor Culture

Charlie Post was 67 years old when called into the ministry. He was encouraged to enroll at CLI by his pastor, Rev. Tom Groelsema, in Byron Center, MI. Charlie was considered too old by many to receive a call, but Tom encouraged him to take that next step. Tom would meet with Charlie along the way to encourage him and share pastoral insights. Charlie got his ministry diploma and he's now preaching at churches, nursing homes and the gospel mission. Tom organized a time where Charlie received his diploma in front of the Elders and Deacons of his church.

Local pastors and church leaders see the doctrine and life of their members close up. These local leaders have made a commitment to bring those in their charge to their next step in ministry preparation, whether that is just teaching a class or, in the case of Charlie Post, encouraging him to receive advanced ministry training.

Christian Leaders Institute is designed to encourage local mentors to help local leaders take that next step. On the application of new students, we ask them to designate a mentor and a local pastor. This lets the student know that they are connected. We find that almost everyone has a local leader to whom they are connected in their ministry journey. CLI considers those local mentors as "adjunct faculty".

We have discovered that most students who do not have a local mentor drop out. Because of this, Christian Leaders Institute includes assignments where the student brings work completed to the local mentor or pastor to discuss. This relationship is very valuable and important in the preparing of a church leader.

Christian Leaders Institute is developing mentor centers where students gather to study (More on this in a later chapter).

2. Accessible and Mission Driven

Because the ministry cost in comparison to traditional ministry training schools is so low, we can make this available to any called leaders, offering the training tuition free of charge. However, even though it's free to the student, it's not easy. Humans have the currency of time or money. We take the money equation out of the mix. Since the Internet platform is so efficient, we are able to make this truly a mission that foundations, individuals, and students can support with a great return for their ministry investment.

The funding model of CLI leverages kingdom resources to make possible free of charge high-quality ministry training.

Some have objected to the "free" part because they feel that people will not value what they do not pay for. The fact is that if someone will not value their ministry training unless they have to pay for it, they should find a place to purchase that training. CLI wants intrinsically called pastors who will value their training simply because they need it. We also find that those leaders, when asked to donate for the training of others, are very willing to help.

The other issue is that if Christian Leaders Institute opened up a tuition department, it would add to overhead, and that cost would prevent CLI from reaching even more leaders to train.

3. Appropriate Academic Expectations

When the Discipleship model re-asserted itself in the 1990s, there was great optimism that this was going to unleash a new age of ministry preparation. The fact was that many were recruited to be pastors, received some training (often in specialized areas like church planting) but these leaders did not get enough of the academic training they needed. The result? Many failed.

The Bible, church, people and their souls, contemporary society, different questions about God and faith, pastoral care, church leadership: these are just some of the areas in which pastors have to be competent and knowledgeable. It is unwise to give newly called leaders barely enough foundational training and hope that they will be successful in ministry.

This attitude of giving a new leader just enough basic training caused many to question their confidence in the discipleship model. Some international ministries recruit church leaders, help them plant a church, report the results to the donors and move on to do this cycle again. These same ministries care little if that leader is trained to be sustainable. Their only concern is that the ministry expectations of their fundraising department are met. In many parts of the world heresies have developed when western culture is more concerned about ministry "results" rather than building a sustainable Christian culture.

Christian Leaders Institute, under the academic leadership of Dr. David Feddes, seeks to give each class the essential academics that a student would get at a seminary, but in such a way that it is contextual for students everywhere.

This model assures that classes are designed which do not require outside books, yet the equivalent of those books is given in the online syllabus. The classes include lectures that can be watched over and over again. The classes include quizzes and papers that hold students accountable to learn the material.

Dr. Feddes is now designing elective courses with legacy material that we have received recently in partnership with other ministries. The late Dr. Francis Schaeffer is being featured in one course. The late Dr. John Stott is featured in another one. The Internet allows all of these intellectual possibilities and more.

The most important thing is that excellent intellectual ministry training is delivered while still preserving the local mentor relationship.

4. Bi-Vocational Sensitivities

We believe that most future church leaders will be bi-vocational church leaders like the apostle Paul. The building of the training cultivation system that supports bi-vocational leaders is a passion at CLI.

CLI is very sensitive to the needs of bi-vocational leaders. We have designed courses to be very friendly for those who already have a job. The courses, while maintaining their academic rigor, can be done with students giving 2-5 hours a week. This allows a full-time working student to still receive ministry training.

The church planting action course assumes that the church planter will be bi-vocational. With funding for missions so small in this culture, church planters need to more and more have the expectation that they are going to have to support themselves in ministry until their church can afford to provide them with a salary.

5. Low Ministry Overhead Oriented

The Internet is like the energy converter box that would change everything if it were invented. The entire school is on the Internet cloud. This is true even to the point that traditional classes are not needed. Offices are not needed. Professors are recruited and recorded. The recordings can be used again and again. Generations of students can receive training. Classes can be constantly tweaked and improved.

Christian Leaders Institute has a getting started class that is designed to replace an admissions department. If a student can get through the getting started class, they are usually able to complete all the courses at CLI (More on this class later).

The Internet has become a game-changer for ministry training. We have an opportunity as the church of God to bring excellent ministry training to mentors and students. They, in turn, will recruit, train and mobilize an army of called and equipped ministry leaders.

CHAPTER 3

CALLING OF REVIVAL LEADERS - GOD CALLS LEADERS

<u>Jeremiah 1:4-5</u> The word of the LORD came to me, saying, "Before I formed you in the womb I knew you, before you were born I set you apart; I appointed you as a prophet to the nations."

"Called" revival leaders are everywhere. They dwell in the slums of Ghana. They minister to people in the inner city of Baltimore. These leaders are called in the most rural places, like 100 miles from Saskatchewan, Canada. These leaders are called in places that actively persecute Christians, like Pakistan and Saudi Arabia. Called leaders are just that, they are called. The vast majority of these leaders do not have formal seminary training, most cannot afford it, even though that training is needed and wanted. These are the leaders that will be used by God to create long term Christian culture.

Rev. David W. Henson, Jr., of White Plains, Maryland, is one of those leaders. David has been serving as a pastor without formal training for over 26 years. He writes:

> I have been married for nineteen years to my wife Connie and we live in White Plains, Maryland. I am a bi-vocational minister. When I am not serving the Lord, I

work as a Service Tech for a home respiratory company. My walk with Jesus started at the age of four when my parents took me to church for the first time. I grew up with a hunger for the Word of God and I have dedicated my life to studying it. At the age of 16, I felt the call of God on my life to serve Him. After many years of studying at the School of Hard Knocks, God opened the door for me to enter the ministry. Over the past 26 years, I have had the honor of serving our Savior as an evangelist, Senior Pastor, Associate Pastor and Youth Pastor.

I remember in my younger days how much I wanted to be a famous pastor or evangelist. I wanted to travel the world for Jesus. But as I matured, I came to the realization that not all of us are called to be used that way. After serving in many capacities for His church, I understood that serving Him went way beyond my wants and desires. My goal as a minister of His glorious gospel is to be used in any way that He sees fit. He is the potter and I am the clay. I want to proclaim the love of Jesus Christ and teach people how they can be victorious in their walk of faith.

David Henson did not minister to people based on what he was going to get out of it. He sensed the call of God. He has ministered for 26 years without formal training. His calling was his ministry currency. He could never afford to get formal training despite the fact that he wanted it and needed it.

The Opportunity

What if the cultivation system for identifying, training and mobilizing Christian leaders to strengthen the church was simplified, but not compromised? What if any called leader could simply talk to their pastor, and their pastor could become their mentor or sponsor? What if high-level Bible School seminary-style education was available free of charge and brought directly to leaders through an Internet connection? What if the system was set up in such a way that strong accountability pieces were hard-wired into the process, so that those who sense the call could be tested in that call? What if the cost to develop all of this was so efficient that we could offer advanced training as a mission where contributions were not lost in residency overhead or in paying tenured professors? What if instead, for a fraction of the cost of traditional Bible schools or seminaries, you could train thousands of called Christian leaders?

Christian Leaders Institute has made major steps in bringing high-level ministry training to called leaders everywhere. This new paradigm for training called leaders has worked. From its beginning with six applications and three active students in 2006, all from the USA, Christian Leaders Institute has grown to an active student body of thousands of students from all over the world.

Getting Started Class

Christian Leaders Institute has a Getting Started Class that allows anyone to explore their calling and test their resolve to receive ministry training for the purpose of bringing revival. Later, I will address the thinking behind the Getting Started Class. Let me just briefly introduce this class to you now.

The first part of the class introduces to students a reproducible walk with God that is the foundation for their ministry readiness. This class is positioned to be a very cost-effective admissions department. If a student can complete this part of the class, Christian Leaders Institute is more assured that these students warrant a scholarship to continue their advanced training. In this first part of the class, the students are invited to finish a donor profile and are granted a tuition scholarship. Students and supporting churches are asked to make donations to the school each semester they study at CLI. Supporters of this concept have enjoyed a great ministry return for their stewardship.

The second part of the course lays out the Christian basics. This is a Christian doctrine class that covers subjects like, the Bible, God, Father, Son and Holy Spirit, Sin, Salvation and much more. When the student completes these two parts of the getting started class they receive the "Christian Basics Certificate." This certificate gives them a good foundation for studying at Christian Leaders Institute.

Students will also find out after taking the Getting Started Class whether the core basics of ministry are right for them. One of the biggest gifts Christian Leaders Institute can give is to weed out those who are not called to be pastors. This Getting Started Class can really help students get a good start or get a good ending to their time at Christian Leaders Institute.

Equipping Called Church Leaders

Many people have asked, "Who are the target leaders CLI is looking to recruit, train and mobilize?" This question has been intensely discussed, and to answer this question we had to dig deep into questions like: what is the church, what is calling, and what are characteristics and qualifications of calling? In the remainder of this chapter and the next one, I am going to share our thoughts about who Christian Leaders Institute is looking to train.

At Christian Leaders Institute we are all about helping the called ones become the sent ones!

The English word "church" comes from the Greek word "EKKLESIA." In ancient Greek that means "called out." It is clear that this word refers to people who were asked to respond to the call of the message. These believers were called to put their faith in Jesus Christ as the Messiah (John 1:41) and the Lord (I Corinthians 1:2) of their lives.

Church leaders themselves were called to put their belief, trust, and faith in Jesus as the seed of all their leadership.

Pastors and church leaders cannot lead where they have not been, and definitely should not be in ministry. The starting point is the actual call to faith, responding to the call of the gospel. If church leaders do not believe that Christ is their passion, they will be ineffective in proclaiming the gospel message and calling others into a relationship with Christ.

The calling of church leaders includes higher expectations for living out the faith and greater responsibility; this is true despite the fact that humans are flawed and sinners. A real walk of faith is foundational if someone senses the call into ministry. This is why the ordination of church leaders has also been done prayerfully and thoughtfully. The Bible cautions against being too quick in the ordaining of office bearers: 1 Timothy 5:22 says, "Do not be hasty in the laying on of hands, and do not share in the sins of others. Keep yourself pure."

Church leaders have a calling by Christ to intentionally order part of their time, actions, and priorities around building the ecclesia, the church.

The offices of elder and deacon were instituted in the early church. The offices of elder and deacon are the foundation of all leadership in the church of Christ. Out of this leadership structure bi-vocational leaders emerge. If someone would not be a worthy elder or deacon, they ought to be very wary about considering a calling into ministry. This is why Christian Leaders Institute puts a premium on local connection, mentorship and sponsorship. If someone senses the call into ministry, the local church members, their leaders and others have seen the truth of their walk and faith. If at a local level, prospective students do not have the confidence of their faith community, those students may want to seriously consider whether God has called them into church ministry.

The truth is that pastors, church planters, and chaplains all fit into the categories of elder and deacon. If prospective future church leaders have the confidence of their local bodies, and they prayerfully sense the calling to be church leaders, the local church should do all it can to train and mobilize those who are called. These called leaders will sustain Christian culture and create more capital.

Let us talk about what goes into knowing whether or not students are called into ministry. What goes into finding out if they are called to be ministry leaders? What follows is a list of seven areas of spiritual practice, as well as discernment insights, that may help students sense the calling of God to lead in ministry. No one is strong in every area, and many of these areas can be developed and cultivated in a person if they are motivated. The apostle Paul exhibited for all time the characteristic of being a "called" church leader.

Characteristics of Called Revival Leaders

Christian Leaders Institute is not just some high technology place where we put classes on the Internet. We are very concerned that everyone who enrolls gets great ministry training. We also hold to the value that everyone who comes to CLI may be called to further ministry. We want called leaders who have counted the cost. Students, donors and supporters keep asking, what type of student do you seek to serve? What are the characteristics of the students you desire at Christian Leaders Institute? What qualifications are you asking of your students? I think those are great questions, and so important that I think we should talk about them.

Here are some of the characteristics of church leaders, whether bi-vocational or vocational. Prospective pastors and leaders need to read these characteristics carefully and prayerfully, in consultation with their spouses, mentors, or pastors. As they consider whether they are "called" to be a pastor, church planter or in any other ministry calling, these are the areas they will want to explore, in addition to the humble walk with God that all believers are called to embody.

While it can be difficult to discern whether or not you are called by God into ministry, at Christian Leaders Institute we want new students to consider these characteristics. In the next chapter, we are going to talk about qualifications. If you are a donor or encourager of Christian Leaders Institute, you will be made more aware of what we are looking for in the called leaders that we are seeking to equip.

Vital Walk with God-inspired Call

First of all, as mentioned earlier, if future leaders are even considering being in ministry, they must have a real walk with God. Further, their "call" and urgency must come to them from God out of that walk. Do they find themselves praying and meditating in his Word regularly? If these potentially called leaders do not care for talking to God or hearing from his Word, they should consider doing something else with their time. Being a church leader is about serving and having a relationship with God. Do they find in their prayer and devotional life that God has placed urgency in their heart for reaching others and helping others reach others? Are these leaders filled with the Holy Spirit?

The apostle Paul often talked about that urgency. He begins his epistle to the Romans,

> *Paul, a servant of Christ Jesus, called to be an apostle and set apart for the gospel of God... (Romans 1:1)*

God still calls people to call others to become leaders of the called community, the church.

Giftedness

Do future leaders have gifts or the potential of developing gifts for being ministry leaders? These prospective leaders should already have some gifts in this area, whether they are an introvert or extrovert. There are many places for ministry service in the church of Christ.

For instance, some students desire to be church planters. A church planter directly plants culture. When someone plants a new church they really plant new culture. Do these potential leaders have gifts for church planting? Are they gifted in starting new organizations? Do they have the gift of self-aware thinking?

These and more are some of the gifts they will need to evaluate where they fit in the "called community." Gifts and competencies cannot be confused. Some may have special gifting in certain areas, but will still need to develop minimal skill in other areas. Leaders can develop competencies in areas that they are not strongly gifted in, and they can grow in areas that they are gifted in. Called leaders do amazing things with or without the complete gift package. They can mobilize and create a stage for others to use their gifts. The apostle Paul made the point that each of us has been given different gifts in the mission.

> *It was he who gave some to be apostles, some to be prophets, some to be evangelists, and some to be pastors and teachers, (Ephesians 4:11)*

Interest

Church leaders know they are called when they are actually interested in the work of the church. Are their life, breath, and love all for building the body of Christ? As they go about their day, do they find themselves thinking of ways to include people in worship, to reach people, to minister to their family and to share God's Word wherever they go? This may seem like an obvious point to make, but it is important as the leader in the church to have this genuine interest in the things of God's church. If this interest is not there, a person may not be called to ministry.

At Christian Leaders Institute, we deal with a lot of church leader types, and we have been involved in planting and pastoring lots of churches. We have noticed that called leaders have urgency about them, similar to what we hear the apostle Paul speaking of in Romans. This interest is vital to a call into church leadership.

> *I will not venture to speak of anything except what Christ has accomplished through me in leading the Gentiles to obey God by what I have said and done — by the power of signs and miracles, through the power of the Spirit. So from Jerusalem all the way around to Illyricum, I have fully proclaimed the gospel of Christ. It has always been my ambition to preach the gospel where Christ was not known, so that I would not be building on someone else's foundation. (Romans 15:19-20)*

Temperament

Future church leaders need temperaments for leadership in the church. Do they deal with failure well? Are they leaders of peace? Church leaders have huge responsibility in the eternal destinies of souls. Will they be able to handle the stress or crack under pressure? People will criticize them. They can easily get caught up into conflicts with those they are calling to faith. Could they learn to deal with their congregation in a compassionate and understanding way?

Over the years we have been tested repeatedly. When we first went into ministry, we were figuring out who we were as leaders. Some prospective leaders have already figured much out about this, while others have much to learn. There will be much testing along the way. Church leaders need to have a temperament of growing when tested. Truly the apostle Paul had that temperament,

> *But we have this treasure in jars of clay, to show that the surpassing power belongs to God and not to us. We are afflicted in every way, but not crushed; perplexed, but not driven to despair; persecuted, but not forsaken; struck down, but not destroyed; always carrying in the body the death of Jesus, so that the life of Jesus may also be manifested in our bodies. (2 Corinthians 4:7-10)*

Humanity

Church leaders are human and they must always identify with their humanity. Some may wonder what is meant by this in relationship to calling into ministry. Are prospective leaders approachable? Are they interesting? Do they read, browse, and watch interesting stuff that the many people they are called to reach interact with? For instance, they might be fans of American football. This ability, to connect with things that people do, will be important for the church leader to relate to them. There are so many honorable things that leaders will hold in common with their parishioners. A prospective Christian leader needs to be relatable in enough ways for them to connect to real people. Church leaders should not come off as boring or irrelevant; instead, they should see everything they do as somehow tying into the calling to call people to put their faith in Christ.   Church leaders are fun, they have a sense of humor, but their humor does not put people down. They can laugh at themselves and do not take themselves too seriously. They can have deep conversations but also enjoy the lighthearted side of things. Church leaders are not afraid to be real; they are open, and people can actually get to know them. They share the truth of their humanity, so that even that humanity itself can serve to lead people to walk with God.

The apostle Paul understood how to be like the people he was reaching, and then became like them. In a striking passage, Paul talks about the osmosis of what occurs when a church leader is connected to his church -- notice how human this is:

> *I plead with you, brothers, become like me, for I became like you. You have done me no wrong. As you know, it was because of an illness that I first preached the gospel to you. Even though my illness was a trial to you, you did not treat me with contempt or scorn. Instead, you welcomed me as if I were an angel of God, as if I were Christ Jesus himself. (Galatians 4:12-14)*

Competency of Lifestyle

Called church leaders are sustainable. Are they basically stable as people? Do they do what they say they will do? Are they truthful? Are they moderate in their life choices? Do they have healthy habits? Do they take care of themselves? Are they hurting about something from their past that still spills over in a major way? Are they bitter about something? They should be sustainable and happy with who they are, where they have been, what they are doing, and where they are going.

The apostle Paul was a very interesting man who was very competent. He supported his ministry by making tents, and he still had time to preach, teach, and heavily contribute to the starting of the Christian movement. In fact, at times his stressing of competency was so strong, people today can misunderstand the apostle Paul.

> For even when we were with you, we gave you this rule: "If a man will not work, he shall not eat." (2 Thessalonians 3:10)

Confirmation

If someone is called into ministry they should have confirmation. They should talk to those who know them best -- their spouse, family, and friends -- about whether or not they could see them as a sustainable church leader. Not having their spouse and family behind them in ministry is a red flag.

It has been said, in the calling of pastors and church planters, that there is an internal call and an external call. The internal call comes out of one's personal piety and walk with God; it includes self-assessment of whether one is called to be in ministry. The external call is others saying that a person is someone who they would hypothetically follow in the calling to faith. The apostle Paul talks about Timothy and often mentions his external calling to ministry,

> *But you know that Timothy has proved himself, because as a son with his father he has served with me in the work of the gospel. (Philippians 2:22)*

Assessing Leaders at Christian Leaders Institute

The calling of God is a work of God-believers. God has built and sustained His church for over 2000 years identifying church leaders this way. It is true that people have misread this calling, run from this calling, and soiled this calling; but this is the way God has established the universal church, which is the oldest organization in the world today.

Christian Leaders Institute wants to remove every unnecessary barrier from prospective ministry candidates. The internal and external callings and all the dynamics associated with them have brought leaders from every nation and tribe ready to be trained for ministry. We want to make their training available and accessible so that hundreds of thousands of leaders are trained for the mission.

You might be reading this book wondering whether you are called into ministry. You might know someone who has mentioned an interest in looking into ministry. We have put together an exercise that will help you or someone you know determine whether a calling is possible. You or the person you know who is interested in ministry should do this exercise with as many people in a local context as possible, but do not pick too many naysayers. (Note: If someone's spouse is a naysayer that will really challenge your ability to lead in ministry). These questions can be done by you or bring them to your friend who has an interest in ministry.

Calling Assessment Exercise

Do you see in me a vital walk or the potential for a vital walk with God?

Do I possess leadership gifts? Would I be able to bless you at a church that I am thinking about starting or giving leadership in?

Do you see in me communication and interpersonal relationship skills that you would find desirable in a leader you would be associated with?

Do you see that I have a hunger for reaching people? Do you see me as on-fire to proclaim the gospel?

Do you see that I really have an interest in reaching people to the point that I would do it for free?

Do you see me as having the temperament of a church leader who will be criticized and not become bitter because of failure and challenges?

Do you see me as someone who is a person of peace who will help others grow?

Do you see me as someone who can take some risks for God?

Do you see me as approachable? Do you see me as open and willing to share?

Do you see me as someone you can relate to?

Do you see me as someone who is stable?

Do you see me as someone who is able to be sustainable as a person and as a leader of others?

Do you affirm that I have a special calling on my life for ministry?

Christian Leaders institute is where ordinary leaders can explore their ministry callings and get the necessary advanced training to do well in ministry.

If you are reading this book as a student, prayerfully consider your calling. In the next chapter, I am going to talk about the qualifications you need to aspire to in becoming a pastor or church leader.

"Calling" is the currency of creating a legacy of revival leaders like Adoniram Judson, or like Hudson Taylor, or like Charles Spurgeon. At Christian Leaders Institute, if Christian leaders are called into ministry, we want to help them get the training they need to do well. This will build the kingdom of God. As you consider CLI, consider that calling into ministry has always been the key issue. Ministry leaders are not at heart rent-a-pastors; God calls them into a most holy calling.

CHAPTER 4

APPROVED REVIVAL LEADERS: QUALIFIED AND READY

> 2 Timothy 2:15 Do your best to present yourself to God as one approved, a workman who does not need to be ashamed and who correctly handles the word of truth.

What do revival leaders look like? Revival leaders are with God. Saved by God from their sin and rebellion through the gospel of Jesus Christ. Revival leaders have the passion for seeing the whole world reached for God.

Revival leaders are <u>to be</u> the part. Revival pastors and church leaders lead people out of who they are. The qualifications of church office bearers are about describing the basic traits that reflect sustainable church leaders in every generation. These qualifications are timeless and must be taken very seriously if someone believes they are called to ministry.

Qualifications are like the beauty college applicant who gets hired because she has the "qualifications" to "minister" to the beauty needs of a certain clientele. If someone is called to be a pastor, church planter, chaplain, or church staff pastor, there are certain qualifications that accompany that calling.

Appropriate To Want to Be a Pastor

Is it appropriate to want to be ordained? That is an

important question. Some will argue that wanting ordination to be a deacon, elder or pastor is not something someone should want to do. Yet the Bible encourages believers to go as far as they can in serving the Lord.

Paul says to Timothy in 1 Timothy 3:1, "Here is a trustworthy saying: If anyone sets his heart on being an overseer, he desires a noble task." If that someone is you and you sense the urgency to serve God in a great capacity, that is something you should explore.

But understand that someone who is a pastor needs to actually "be the part." We want people at Christian Leaders Institute who are the part. Let's reflect on this for a while. Understand that when leaders look at their qualifications to be a leader in the church it can be overwhelming and they could easily conclude that they are not perfect or together enough to set their hearts on being church leaders.

Leaders should not be overwhelmed, instead leaders ought to be energized in these qualifications. I will go so far as to say, if these qualifications are not generally present and the leader does not want to aspire to be these qualifications, that potential leader is not called into ministry.

Qualifications of Called Revival Leaders

As we talk about the qualifications for being an office bearer, the first thing to realize is that some of these qualifications are very objective; some are discipleship qualifications and maturity qualifications, and you will not meet these qualifications perfectly.

You may find that you are stronger in certain areas than in

other areas. Yet your life must reflect that you are a real work-in-progress in your desire to be a leader in the church.

Here are the characteristics of elders and pastors as found in 1 Timothy 3:2-7. Revival leaders share these qualifications.

1. Leaders Who Stay Out of Trouble

"Not arrested" is the literal Greek translation. "Not arrested" could be an objective qualification, but the key question here is how are you staying out of trouble in areas that will hurt the gospel ministry. In other words, are you keeping sinful practices away from you? Are you seeking to be well respected by your community of residence? If you have a reputation for greedy or immoral activity in your community and people can come forward presently to accuse you of shady activities, you may want to think again about being a pastor. This is not to say that you may have struggled in the past and you are forever barred from ministry, just that your past needs to be addressed. Christian leaders who have gone through divorce need to have repented of any sin involved with the divorce and been restored into a healthy walk with God before they should consider being a pastor or leader in the church.

2. Leaders Who Do Not Practice Polygamy

Polygamy was practiced in Bible times, and it was present in the early church. Polygamy was practiced by many of the converts from Judaism - especially the wealthy. And while these new converts to Christianity may have continued to practice polygamy, office bearers and pastors were disqualified for participating in this practice. We don't know all the reasons why this was included as an objective qualification, but it was. Both elders and deacons were to "be the husband of but one wife" This is not referring here to those who have been restored after a divorce or death of a spouse and now are remarried. This is referring to polygamy.

3. Leaders Who Are Sober or Temperate in Attitude

This qualification is not talking about drunkenness; that topic is still to come. This qualification has to do with judgment. Are you circumspect in your reasoning? Are you balanced in how you evaluate yourself and others? If you "always" jump to conclusions, if you are "too positive or too negative", that is something you want to be aware of as you learn ways to be more balanced.

4. Leaders Who Exhibit Moderation

The Greek word in this qualification literally means, "safe mind." Leaders who exhibit this qualification are self-controlled in their actions, opinions and speech. These leaders realize that they need to hold their counsel at times. In their personal life, they need to keep their sinful nature surrendered to Christ, understanding that they too are not perfect. Leaders like this enjoy life, but to the point that any one thing in creation does <u>not</u> own them other than Christ.

5. Leaders Who Act Orderly and Respectable

The Greek word here comes from the word *Kosmos* which means literally "order." Christian leaders who are called into the pastorate have that certain orderly and respectable trait to them. For instance, are you on time or are you habitually late to meetings? Is your dress appropriate for those that you are called to reach? Do people respect your opinion?

6. Leaders Who Are Friendly to Everyone

This Greek word is a combination of two words. The first word, *filos*, means friend. The second word means people, strangers, foreigners. Leaders called into the ministry are friendly and welcoming to people that are currently not part of the group. Many times this is considered by some to not be as important a character trait, yet this has everything to do with character. Hospitality is about showing someone love... even someone you do not know.

7. Leaders Who Are Willing to Teach or Mentor

Many times leaders think that this refers to teaching or preaching at a program or a worship service. There are lots of ways to teach or mentor. Church leaders see the need to pass on the lifestyle and the faith of Christianity. If you are called to be a pastor, this qualification very much applies to you. If you are a preacher you will take this very seriously in your calling. This qualification means that you will always be walking with God, learning his Word and sharing what your walk and learning brings to others.

8. Leaders Who Are Not Given to Addictions

This Greek word specifically talks about "wine," literally "not near wine," referring to drunkenness. This needs to be taken metaphorically as well. Pastors and church planters have to stay away from addictive behavior. This is challenging because addictive behavior comes in many sizes and colors. Many pastors have struggled over the centuries with various addictions. It seems like the evil one attacks in this area ferociously. The common addictions today have a lot to do with what technology brings into society.

Many leaders are addicted to entertainment, video games, pornography, and/or Internet browsing. Other leaders have struggled with substance abuse, using wine, beer, and even drugs. Addictions can also include food, shopping, clothing, etc. Future pastors and leaders have to take the matter of addictions very seriously and set up accountability and support so that they are not mastered by sin or anything else in God's creation. Remember 1 Corinthians 6:12, "'Everything is permissible for me' — but not everything is beneficial. 'Everything is permissible for me' — but I will not be mastered by anything."

9. Leaders Who Are Not Violent

The Greek word used here literally means "not a striker." It means someone who is not given to violent outbursts or angry blasts. Pastors and leaders are not given to revenge or payback. Hate and anger are not the operating system of a pastoral personality. Have you ever seen a pastor or leader exhibit a violent outrage? This outrage will bring harm to their ministry more than it will make some point to the person they offended.

10. Leaders Who Are Not Greedy Misers

The literal meaning of the Greek word here is "base or selfish gain." In other words, leaders who are solely motivated by what they get financially or in other forms of repayment are not qualified to be pastors. While the apostle Paul writes that the worker deserves his wages, there is a fine line here between career and calling. You should not become a pastor because you think it is a nice job where you will get paid well. This is a calling and you cannot think of this calling as a career. Instead, you are to be motivated out of generosity and realize that God will cover all your needs as you are a good steward of what He gives you.

11. Leaders Who Are Self-Aware in Their Gentleness

The Greek word here is "appropriate." By implication this word is translated as gentle, mild, or patient. We need to add one more dimension to that word and that dimension is self-awareness in your responses. In every relationship and in every church things will happen and maybe even offensive words will be said to you. Many times someone will treat the pastor in a way that gives the pastor a clue of what is needed. For instance, if someone is unfairly critical of the pastor, this is likely how he treats his family. This gives you great insight in to how to give pastoral care to that family and that person. Remember the axiom, how someone treats you is how he likely treats others in his life.

12. Leaders Who Love Peace

Some people have to win every fight and be right about every issue. This does not make a good pastor. While some fights are very important to win, most fights are not worth the time required to get involved. The apostle Paul encourages us to live at peace with others. He writes in Romans 12:18, "If it is possible, as far as it depends on you, live at peace with everyone."

As a called pastor, you must be very careful as you lead people to peace. Some pastors exert control to bring unity on an issue by telling parishioners that God has led them to this opinion or position. Be very careful about leading as an ambassador of God, making sure you really desire peace, not just the appearance of peace.

13. Leaders Who Are Not Covetous

This is a "killer" in ministry. The Greek word here means "wishing for more silver." It refers to thoughts and desires that will sink your ministry calling. The fact is that you will never have enough money. You will never have the perfect church; you will never have the perfect family or spouse. Where you are now may not be as good as where you were a year ago. Imagining that the future may be better than now may not help you. Effective Christian leaders are content even while they are seeking to improve. Called leaders are to be content in who they are and where they are. It is from that contentment that they can determine if they should take another church or do something else. They are not motivated by the "grass is greener over there" attitude. Whether it is with silver or something else, effective pastors are content in Christ.

14. Leaders who Lead in Their Homes and Are Respected

The issues of leadership are a microcosm of the issues of leadership in any church setting. If you are able to give appropriate leadership in your family, including your spouse, this will directly translate in the church.

If your children do not see in you that you are a Biblical leader who commands respect, people outside your family will have a hard time seeing that as well. All the issues of your leadership have a foundation in your family. Someone's reputation in their family is huge in how they will be received in the church. The apostle Paul even quips, "If anyone does not know how to manage his own family, how can he take care of God's church?" (1 Timothy 3:5)

15. Leaders Who are Settled in Their Walk and Doctrine

The apostle Paul observed many early leaders that fell away from the faith. If you are called into ministry you want to be settled in your walk and in your doctrine. Paul writes in 1 Timothy 3:6, "He must not be a recent convert, or he may become conceited and fall under the same judgment as the devil." When you are unsettled in your walk or doctrine, you are open for attitudes and ideas that leave the Biblical worldview.

If you or your spouse are a recent convert, go slowly into pursuing your ministry calling. Later in 1 Timothy 3, the apostle Paul encourages that deacons be tested. "They must keep hold of the deep truths of the faith with a clear conscience. They must first be tested; and then if there is nothing against them, let them serve as deacons." (1 Timothy 3:9-10)

Leaders need to be tested. Where have you been tested? How have you done? What did you learn?

16. Leaders Who Are Respected in Their Community of Relationships

The same principle applies here that applies with a leader's family. If someone is interacting with people and they see that that leader is fair and honest, this is an indicator that this person could be qualified to be a pastor. On the other hand, if the community has experienced that the leader treats people badly, one would question if the person is ready to be a pastor or church leader.

Assessment

If you are a new or potential student at Christian Leaders Institute, I want you to prayerfully read each of these 15 qualifications and to develop an honest assessment of where you are now. Then I encourage you to develop a plan to grow in these qualifications. You will never be perfect, but a teachable attitude led by God's grace, His Word and Spirit will transform you into a Christian leader who will be used by God to change the world. Have your spouse, mentor, sponsor or trusted friend, go over each one of these qualifications with you. Aspire to BE these qualifications.

Ordination and Christian Leaders Institute

Thousands of Christian Leaders Institute students have been seeking ordination. CLI students come from various traditions and have various understandings of many topics concerning ordination, such as: Who can be ordained? What roles can women be ordained into? How does someone get ordained?

Christian Leaders Institute recognizes that we are training Christian leaders and giving them the best possible ministry training so that they can minister in their local context. This means that our professors will share their scriptural convictions guided by our Statement of Faith. We recognize that there will not be complete agreement about many issues including tongues, end times, and ordinations. We are going to look at the basic Biblical and practical insights that inform those who are sensing the call to ministry and ordination.

What is Ordination?

The definition of ordination is different for those in different church traditions. Ordination to the Catholics, Anglicans, Methodists, Lutherans and other high ordination denominations are primarily connected to Christian leaders or hierarchy already in place. These leaders appoint new leaders who have demonstrated calling, gifts and competency. Ordination to Presbyterian and Reformed denominations are much more connected to elder assemblies. Ordination in the Baptist, Assemblies, Congregational, non-denominational, house church movement and other more grass-roots authority traditions see ordination as coming out of the democratic structure of the authority of the group. Ordination to many is defined as a certificate of ordination, which is a local certification that organizations give leaders for their credibility.

Christian Leaders Institute Goals

Christian Leaders Institute seeks to equip called leaders to be ready for their ordination. If they already are ordained, our goal is to better equip them for effective service in their ministry position. We have a "bloom where you are planted" approach to training Christian leaders. Leaders come to us with a calling to minister, our goal is to help them get ready.

The last two chapters dealt with the "who" of the leaders we seek to train at Christian Leaders Institute. Being a church leader means being a called leader who has the qualifications to honorably discharge the duties of one of God's servants. We are looking for leaders whose calling and qualifications converge together to characterize the leaders who will proclaim the gospel. While no one is perfect in every way, called and qualified leaders are the ones Christian Leaders Institute seeks to train.

If you are reading this book as a student and the last two chapters substantially characterize you, we welcome you to start your training at Christian Leaders Institute. CLI takes each leader's calling, character, and qualifications very seriously.

Christian Leaders Institute is looking to train called ministry leaders who embody the characteristics of inspiring leaders. We are also seeking to train qualified leaders who are the part. These goals of assessment can be difficult to accomplish and we are convinced that we will not do it as well as we want to, but we will keep adjusting our program and working toward effectively identifying, training and mobilizing called Christian leaders in mentor relationships. In the next chapter, we are going to look at how the Getting Started Class is a great introduction to ministry training and a test that separates the called from those that are just checking out ministry training.

CHAPTER 5

STUDYING REVIVAL LEADERS: START WITH A GETTING STARTED CLASS

<u>2 Peter 1:2-3</u> Grace and peace be yours in abundance through the knowledge of God and of Jesus our Lord. His divine power has given us everything we need for life and godliness through our <u>knowledge of him</u> who called us by his own glory and goodness.

When I was visiting Kenya, Africa in the year 2000, I happened on a newspaper, and I noticed that many young people were dying of AIDS. I expressed my sadness that this terrible sexually transmitted disease was ravishing so many young people, whether they were Christians or non-Christians. I asked a local Christian leader his opinion about this tragedy. In response, he gave me a history lesson I have never forgotten.

I don't remember the various dates he mentioned, but I remember that he said when the missionaries from the developing western nations came to evangelize, they were connected to money, power, and medicine. As they proclaimed the gospel it was very hard to separate the claims of the gospel from the expectations of the imperial nations that controlled the land. For instance, to be a

Christian meant certain western expectations of modest clothing accompanied conversion. To be a Christian included dietary issues. Many "high church" western hymns replaced the indigenous sounds of the native land.

The result was that many Christians had a hard time distinguishing the root of gospel faith from the fruits of gospel faith. In other words, the call of faith was too wrapped up in the western culture. Over time, to be "Christian" entailed a whole package of external behaviors or morality. The core relationship with God and the doctrines of Scripture were replaced with religion and behaviors.

But what does AIDS have to do with fruit and root confusion? That Christian leader in Kenya said that the message many in his country reproduced over generations was a very shallow faith that did little to really restrain sensual indulgence. He went on to say that Christianity was the "breast cover up" religion but not the faith that changes hearts. With hearts unchanged, sensual indulgence was not put in check. So-called "Christians" were just as immoral as non-Christians; they were just more outwardly modest.

This really made me think. When we proclaim the call to faith, are we proclaiming the gospel that changes humans at the root level, that is their hearts? Or are we proclaiming a gospel that changes social structures, so that at the end of the day we confuse the call of the gospel faith? I want to be very clear here that I do believe that the call of the gospel in the hearts of believers will have powerful fruit that will change culture, but we all have to be clear about what the root is and what the fruits are. We have to be very clear about what we are proclaiming as we introduce the call of faith.

What are you called to proclaim? You are called to proclaim the gospel. Those that hear and believe will be saved and are part of the family of God. Church leaders lead or form a "hear the call-to-faith organization," this organization is called the church. The church leader is calling people to believe the message that will change their destiny. When people respond to the message with faith, they are actually born again. Even the faith itself comes from hearing the message. *"Consequently, faith comes from hearing the message, and the message is heard through the word of Christ." (Romans 10:17)*

Church leaders are asking people to put their faith in Christ as their Lord and Savior. They are asking people to be God-centric and not man-centric. They are asking people to order their entire lives around their walk with God, guided by his Word. They are asking people to come back to God and each other as the Bible encourages and commands. They are asking for real revival to God.

Recently, I received a note from one of our African students. He writes about the misconceptions that Africans have about God. What fascinated me about this note is that many Africans have come to believe that all religions are the same. I would venture to say that most people think that religions are about rules and morality, but this student got it right. It has always been about a heart connected to the Father through Jesus. Here is what Moses wrote me:

> Hi Henry,
>
> In the country where I live, some people have a lot of misconceptions about God, the role and personality of Jesus. It's unfortunate that many even do not see the difference between Rastafarianism, Islam, Christianity, and the African Traditional Religion among others. It's common to hear people say that 'all roads lead to Rome,' meaning that all religions lead to heaven/God, but I believe that no one gets to the Father except through Jesus Christ.

Church leaders are going after the heart, the will, and the soul to restore humans into a forgiven relationship with Christ, won for us by the sacrifice of Christ on the cross and the victory of Christ over death in His resurrection. They are asking hearts to believe in Jesus as their Lord and Savior. *"Therefore, holy brothers, who share in the heavenly calling, <u>fix</u> your thoughts on Jesus, the apostle and high priest whom we confess."* (Hebrews 3:1) *" For the word of the cross is folly to those who are perishing, but to us who are being saved it is the power of God. "* (1 Corinthians 1:18)

Church leaders need to be very careful to proclaim the root of faith and then call people to the faith that changes hearts from the inside out. Over the years, I have found that I have always needed to be clear about what we are actually inviting people into when they enter a relationship with Christ. What is the root?

At Christian Leaders Institute we believe the root is a living relationship with God -- Father, Son, and Holy Spirit. We are very careful about laying the foundation for the "knowledge of God.' We are not giving people merely "Religious Training."

At Christian Leaders Institute we have a getting started procedure that starts with students identifying whether they are called into ministry. If they are existing pastors, this class seeks to strengthen and revive their calling.

The second part of this procedure or class is about relational knowledge that includes what we call walking with God. This walking includes prayer and devotional Bible reading and the habits that are associated with that daily walk. This relationship walk is to be reproducible through evangelism.

The third part of this procedure or class is doctrinal. There is also another kind of knowing of God that is included in "walking" with God, and this is the doctrinal knowledge. Both these types of knowing God are very important. At Christian Leaders Institute, this three-part procedure or class is the foundational class that students take that launches them into the rest of their ministry training. This chapter will reveal the DNA of Christian Leaders Institute's foundational Getting Started Class.

As we plant and support Christianity worldwide, we have to be very clear that we build on the root of the gospel and do not promote the fruit as the essence of our faith. The fruit of the faith comes out of the root. We have a Getting Started Class that seeks to help students start their education on the foundation of the walk and thought of the knowledge of God. Let me show you now in more detail how the Getting Started Class works.

Welcome Aboard

Called leaders from around the world find out about Christian Leaders Institute from many sources, including organic optimization, Google Ads, Internet, or organizational referrals and word of mouth. They then go to our website and fill out an application for enrollment. Once this is completed, they are placed into the Getting Started Class.

The Getting Started Class gives people the opportunity to explore whether they are candidates for ministry training at Christian Leaders Institute. Our goal is that students will finish this class and move on, becoming active students earning certificates and diplomas. This class replaces the overhead of an admissions department and eliminates those who are not serious or able to study at Christian Leaders Institute.

The class is divided into three parts and students will be awarded 7 credits and receive the Christian Basics Certificate when they complete the class.

First Part of the Getting Started Class:

The first part of the class is about understanding the vision and culture of online ministry training and the student's calling into the ministry. This part of the class uses and studies this book.

Second Part of the Getting Started Class:

In this second part of the class, students learn or review the essence of a walk with God. They learn how a walk with God includes reproducibly talking to God (prayer) and listening to God (Bible reading) in a repeated way. Students learn these reproducible faith-formation habits and how to share them in evangelism.

These habits are taught to students in the Seven Connections, which outline a reproducible walk with God that includes the student's personal life, marriage, family, friends, public worship, kingdom, and world.

Lectures in video format are shared with students. The students take quizzes that are automatically graded to make sure that they actually engage with the materials. Our Internet tools notice whether the students read the materials and watch the videos.

Third Part of the Getting Started Class:

The third part of the class features the teachings of Dr. Edwin Roels. Not only has Dr. Roels been the president of Kuyper College, a pastor in a local church, and an executive leader at the Bible League; he is also a skilled theological communicator. Dr. David Feddes, CLI provost, has taken Dr. Roels' Christian Basics material and created a class including video lectures that lays an excellent foundation for the doctrines of the faith.

Students are quizzed after each topic and the topics are historic key doctrinal topics including:

The Bible
God
Creation
Jesus Christ
Salvation
The Holy Spirit
Christian Living
Suffering and Persecution
The Future

Students learn these truths and more, find where they are taught in Scripture, and grow in their ability to state Christian truths clearly and concisely to others.

Characteristics of the Getting Started Class

The first characteristic of the Getting Started Class is to reveal academic competency. The Getting Started Class is designed in such a way that if a student can complete these classes and pass the quizzes, they have the essential academic skills necessary to succeed at the rest of the curriculum.

Academic training is important. Christian Leaders Institute seeks to not only to give practical ministry insights, but also training which is intellectually stimulating. This prepares our students to become life-long learners of intellectual insights. We tailor our classes to different learning styles. Our classes also take into account that many of our students have English as a second language.

The second characteristic of the Getting Started Class is to reveal technological competency. This class is designed to check out the Internet connections and the technological skills of the students. Everything "technologically" that happens in the Getting Started Class tests whether the students will be able to complete the CLI program. As the Internet continues to penetrate the globe, more and more students will have the technology know-how to succeed.

We have students who have high-speed Internet connections even in the most remote places. Whether in rural Jamaica or urban Nairobi, Kenya, students have access to this training. In many places of the globe, students have computers and Internet before they have clean water.

The Getting Started Class teaches even the most technologically illiterate students basic computer skills. Many of the CLI students have been taught the skills that help them do well in their country as they navigate newer technology that has yet to reach most citizens in their country. CLI is a real blessing for our students.

The third characteristic of the Getting Started Class reveals the commitment level of a student. There is nothing like the three substantial parts of the class that test whether someone is serious about their ministry calling. This Getting Started Class separates those students who really want ministry training from those who are just toying with the idea. This is very important in a mission that is seeking to keep expenses low. We do not want to utilize resources on those who are not called, qualified and committed to do the work needed.

The fourth characteristic of the Getting Started class is the introduction to the way we learn together at Christian Leaders Institute. Students are introduced to staff of Christian Leaders Institute via video. Students are introduced to the culture of CLI, including the mentorship expectations. Frequently asked questions are raised and answered in this class. There are videos that explain the curriculum and videos that explain the admissions process.

As part of learning about our CLI culture, students are introduced to the global identity of Christian Leaders Institute. They find out about our "Chat" feature whereby students can talk to each other. Students are introduced to opportunities to make a donation to Christian Leaders Institute. When a student completes the Getting Started

Class, they have connected with the curriculum, some professors, chatting, and giving.

The fifth characteristic of the Getting Started Class is that students receive their first certificate.

As students complete their Getting Started Class they reach their first graduate level, called Christian Basics. This certificate recognizes the accomplishment of completing the first certificate level.

The student will construct a profile that includes the student's story and their ministry dream. This profile can be shared on our website if security is not an issue for the student.

After students complete the Getting Started Class, they are free to take any classes they desire to take and earn any diploma they are called to earn.

CHAPTER 6

TRAINING REVIVAL LEADERS: EFFECTIVE COURSE OF STUDY

One of the most exciting but also tragic revival leaders was Evan Roberts. Evan Roberts was used by God to usher in the Welsh Revival of the early nineteen hundreds. He grew up in a devout Welsh home with thirteen other children. From a young age he sought after God. He often would actively share Scriptures with his friends and co-workers at the coal mine.

A visiting evangelist named Seth Joshua led a meeting where he asked God to "bend us" to serve God and bring revival to the nations. Evan asked if that revival would happen in him first. He asked for the anointing of the Holy Spirit. He asked God to "bend me". Evan experienced an outpouring of the Holy Spirit. This young man had his heart at a surrendered place and the Great Welsh revival was started.

Evan Roberts was speaking and leading revivals throughout villages and cities. Roberts was passionate in proclaiming sincere devotion to God. He did not trust the traditional places of ministry training such as seminaries. He was concerned that either they were spiritually dead or they would douse the flame of the Holy Spirit.

Evan Roberts started a revival that was felt throughout the world. "Within 2 months of its beginnings there had been over 30,000 converts. Within six months 100,000 converts. By the beginning of 1906 who could know? By 1910 its influence was felt in every corner of the globe".(http://www.pentecostalpioneers.org/ EvanRobertsWelshRevival.html)

The tragic thing about Evan Roberts is that his fear of getting traditional ministry training at a seminary actually ended in hurting him as a revival leader. He did not find a way to get orthodox Biblical ministry training even in alternative ways. The lack of grounded orthodox views sidelined him as a revival leader. Tony Cauchi at Revival – Library wrote about Evan Roberts,

> The revival spread like wildfire all over Wales. Other leaders also experienced the presence of God. Hundreds of overseas visitors flocked to Wales to witness the revival and many took revival fire back to their own land. But the intense presence began to take its toll on Evan. He became nervous and would sometimes be abrupt or rude to people in public meetings. He openly rebuked leaders and congregations alike.
>
> Though he was clearly exercising spiritual gifts and was sensitive to the Holy Spirit, he became unsure of the "voices" he was hearing. Then he broke down and withdrew from public meetings. Accusation and criticism followed and further physical and emotional breakdown ensued.

Understandably, converts were confused. Was this God? Was Evan Roberts God's man or was he satanically motivated? He fell into a deep depression and in the spring of 1906 he was invited to convalesce at Jessie Penn-Lewis' home at Woodlands in Leicester.

It is claimed that Mrs. Penn Lewis used Evan's name to propagate her own ministry and message. She supposedly convinced him he was deceived by evil spirits and, over the next few years co-authored with Evan "War on the Saints", which was published in 1913. This book clearly delineates the confusion she had drawn Evan into. It left its readers totally wary of any spiritual phenomena of any kind or degree. Rather than giving clear guidelines regarding discerning satanic powers, it brought into question anything that may be considered, or that might be described, as Holy Spirit activity. Within a year of its publication, Evan Roberts denounced it, telling friends that it had been a failed weapon which had confused and divided the Lord's people.

Evan stayed at the Penn-Lewis' home for eight years, giving himself to intercession and private group counseling. Around 1920 Evan moved to Brighton and lived alone until he returned to his beloved Wales, when his father fell ill in 1926. He began to visit Wales again and eventually moved there in 1928 when his father died.

Nothing much is known of the years that followed. Evan finally died at the age of 72 and was buried behind Moriah Chapel on Jan 29th 1951.

(http://www.revival-library.org/pensketches/revivalists/robertse.html)

Roberts had burned out. But also he did not have the ministry foundation of solid training in the sound teaching of Scripture to keep his doctrine and life balanced.

Well-Grounded Revival Leaders

What would have happened if Evan Roberts would have had ministry training that kept him walking in the Spirit, but very solid in his doctrine and life? We will never know, but what we do see over and over again is that sound knowledge of key Biblical teachings is important.

Revival leaders are not only filled with the zeal of the Holy Spirit but understand what they believe and why. They need enough ministry training that they can stand many tests of their doctrine and life.

The Apostle Paul illustrated the importance of sound doctrine many times. Here are some samples of what he said,

1 Timothy 1:3   As I urged you when I went into Macedonia, stay there in Ephesus so that you may command certain men not to teach false doctrines any longer.

1 Timothy 4:6-7   If you point these things out to the brothers, you will be a good minister of Christ Jesus, brought up in the truths of the faith and of the good teaching that you have followed. Have nothing to do with godless myths and old wives' tales; rather, train yourself to be godly.

1 Timothy 6:3 If anyone teaches false doctrines and does not agree to the sound instruction of our Lord Jesus Christ and to godly teaching, **4** he is conceited and understands nothing.

2Timothy 4:2 Preach the Word; be prepared in season and out of season; correct, rebuke and encourage—with great patience and careful instruction. **3** For the time will come when men will not put up with sound doctrine.

Titus 1:8-9 Rather he must be hospitable, one who loves what is good, who is self-controlled, upright, holy and disciplined. He must hold firmly to the trustworthy message as it has been taught, so that he can encourage others by sound doctrine and refute those who oppose it.

Titus 2:1 You must teach what is in accord with sound doctrine.

Christian Leaders Institute has put together a curriculum of study that covers the major bases of a solid seminary education. Revival leaders can lead in bringing people back to God wherever they live. We will bring solid Bible based training to support them as sustainable leaders who will stand the various tests that can shipwreck leaders.

The Christian Leaders Curriculum

Since giving solid doctrine to new leaders is very important, I want to be very clear about the doctrinal perspective that guides the formation of our teaching materials. We are guided by a carefully prepared curriculum for the teaching of solid ministry training.

What is a curriculum? The word "curriculum" is Latin and, literally translated, means "race course." There were many around the early 1900s who focused on what curricula (the plural form of curriculum) should be taught. One such man was John Franklin Bobbitt, who was part of the era of Henry Ford and Dale Carnegie. This was the era of efficiency, where everyone was challenged to be their very best and waste was to be eliminated. Bobbitt was sent by the USA to do social engineering in the Philippines. The American leaders wanted more of the social capital of "efficiency" of that era to drive Philippine culture. They planned to accomplish this through an elementary school curriculum designed by Bobbitt. Thus, Bobbitt designed a curriculum that he felt would pass on those American values to the children of the Philippine culture. A curriculum, then, is really the teacher's "canon" of what should be taught to the next generation. Curricula are very important.

It is also important to realize that every curriculum is constructed out of a world-view. John Dewey, another curriculum creator, believed in a world without God. He believed that the true "god" was scientific observation and the "pastors" of society were the teachers in the public school, so he designed a curriculum that separated science from religion and held science to be superior. John Dewey's curriculum was very centered on a community of democracy as the ideal. We can see why he is still very popular.

Curricula, which form the content taught by the leaders, are themselves formed to ingrain in students certain ideals foundational to their worldview perspective. We as church leaders have as our foundation the Bible, and the Bible applies to all generations. However, if we look at the history of the church, we will notice that the curriculum that the leaders used did change. They replaced the early church curriculum with a tradition-laden curriculum that taught that the church organization, and not Jesus and His Word, was the final authority on salvation and life.

New curricula were developed at the time of the Reformation that proclaimed that people had a direct connection to God and were saved by God's grace, through faith, and supported by the church as a called body of believers. The hierarchy of the church was re-thought by the Protestants. New curricula were written and taught to the leaders which reflected the return to a Bible based perspective.

We have many examples of curricula developed throughout history, but what makes a good curriculum? A Christian curriculum comes from a God-honoring worldview. This worldview builds upon God's Word, the Bible, as the only foundation and rule of life and teaching. At CLI, we believe all the core doctrines in a good Christian curriculum must be supported by the Bible. But what are the important points of Christianity? The historic doctrines of the church taught in the Ecumenical creeds like the Apostle's Creed, the Nicene Creed, and the Athanasian Creed.

Reformation Revival Curriculum

The Reformation of the 16th century was a seismic shift back to the Bible in how someone related to God. The Catholic Church of that time had drifted a long way from its Biblical roots. The Reformation brought back doctrines that were grounded in Scripture. Themes of the Reformation included "sola scriptura" (by Scripture alone), "sola fides" (by faith alone), "solus Christus" (through Christ alone), and "soli Deo Gloria" (glory to God alone).
(http://www.theopedia.com/Five_Solas)

The Reformation in the sixteenth century gave renewed clarity to the power of the infallible Scriptures. It established solid teachings that are to be passed down generation after generation. It is out of this Reformation culture that the Christian Leaders Institute Statement of Faith is declared. The themes of Reformation guide the entire curriculum at CLI.

This statement of doctrine forms the kernel of what is taught in ministry training at CLI.

Christian Leaders Institute
Statement of Faith

1. The Bible is God's inerrant Word, the only final authority for faith and life.
   (Proverbs 30:5-6; Isaiah 8:20; John 10:35; 2 Timothy 3:16-17; 2 Peter 1:21)

2. God is Trinity, an eternal, loving unity of three divine Persons: Father, Son, and Holy Spirit. (Deuteronomy 6:4; Matthew 28:19; John 14:26; 2 Corinthians 13:14)

3. God created the universe ex nihilo, from nothing, and made all things very good.
   (Genesis 1-2; Exodus 20:11; Hebrews 11:3)

4. God created humanity to glorify and enjoy God and to be stewards of creation.
   (Genesis 1:26-28; Psalm 8; Isaiah 43:7; Revelation 4:11; Psalm 37:4)

5. Humanity has fallen into sin, and we are totally unable to save ourselves.
   (Genesis 3; Romans 3:12, 23; Romans 5:12)

6. Jesus Christ is fully God and fully man.
   (Matthew 1:21-23; John 1:1,14; 20:28; Hebrews 1:1-4, 2:14)

7. Jesus was born of a virgin, obeyed God perfectly, worked great miracles, died on a cross, rose from the dead, ascended to heaven, and reigns over all things.
   (Luke 1:26-35, Hebrews 4:15; John 14:11, Luke 23-24, Ephesians 1:20-23)

8. Salvation is merited only by Jesus' perfect obedience and substitutionary atonement.
   (Isaiah 53; Hebrews 7:26-27; 2 Corinthians 5:21; Acts 4:12)

9. Salvation is entirely God's gift, not our achievement, and is received by faith, not works. (John 3:16; Romans 1:16-17; Galatians 2:16-21)

10. The Holy Spirit gives new birth, unites us to Christ, equips us with His gifts, and empowers us to be His ambassadors. (John 3:3-8; Romans 8:9-11; Ephesians 3:16-21; 1 Corinthians 12; Acts 1:8)

11. The church is the one body of God's people throughout all generations and from all nations. (Romans 12:5; Galatians 3:26-29; Ephesians 1:22-23; Revelation 7:9)

12. Christ gives two signs and seals of his grace: baptism and the Lord's Supper.
    (John 4:1; 1 Corinthians 12:13; Matthew 28:19; Mark 14:22-24; 1 Corinthians 11:23-26)

13. God's holy angels defend and help God's people. (Psalm 34:7, 91:11; Matthew 18:10; Hebrews 1:14)

14. Satan and other fallen angels are dangerous but doomed. Christ is victor.
    (Ephesians 6:10-18; Colossians 2:15; 1 Peter 5:8; Revelation 12:10-12)

15. Christ will return visibly to rule the world and to make

all things new.
(Matthew 24:30; 1 Thessalonians 4:16; Revelation 21:1-5)

16. God's people will rejoice forever in heaven; God's enemies will suffer forever in hell.
(Daniel 12:2-3; Matthew 25:31-46; Revelation 22:1-5; 2 Thessalonians 1:9)

17. God's covenant addresses not only individuals but also their families.
(Genesis 17:7; 18:19; Deuteronomy 7:9; Joshua 24;15; Psalm 103:17; Acts 11:14; 16:15,31)

18. As individuals, as couples, and as families, we need daily conversation with God through Bible reading and prayer. (Psalm 1; Daniel 6:10; Deuteronomy 6:4-9; Ephesians 6:18; 1 Thessalonians 5:17)

19. We are called to a life of love, as depicted in the Ten Commandments.
(Exodus 20:1-17; Mark 12:30-31; John 14:15; Romans 13:8-10; 1 Corinthians 13)

20. We are called to spread the gospel to people who don't yet follow Christ.
(Psalm 96:3; Matthew 5:14; 28:18-20; 1 Peter 3:15)

21. We are called to a worldview and way of life which seeks to honor Christ in every area of thought and action. (Psalm 24:1; Colossians 3:17; 2 Corinthians

10:5)

Christian Leaders Institute takes our curriculum very seriously. Our belief statement reflects those doctrines and teachings that we believe are most foundational to Christianity. It is founded on Scripture. And it is inspired by the historic church creeds of the faith, especially post-Reformation. Christian Leaders Institute is taking the ancient teachings and putting them on the web so that called future ministry leaders will be able to reproduce these teachings and a godly walk to those people whom God calls them to lead.

The curriculum of CLI is focused to build from and on the Christian capital of the past, addressing the critical issues that leaders face today. What is interesting to me is that I believe we are going back to themes that were very relevant in the early church. Clement of Rome spoke to the same issue as he addressed the Corinthians.

Christian Leaders Program of Study (as of September 2013)

Christian Leaders Institute is developing a ministry training program where outside textbooks are not required for ministry training. We are offering more and more classes where all digital, video and quizzing resources are in the syllabus. Our goal is to eventually have all our courses with the resources necessary contained on the web via downloadable videos, digital context and on-line quizzes.

1. Christian Basics Certificate (7 credits)

Students enter Christian Leaders Institute (CLI) via our Getting Started Class: Reproducible Walk with God and Christian Basics (7 credits). This class introduces students to a reproducible walk with God and grounding in historic Christian doctrine. This class gives them orientation to CLI. After they complete the Getting Started Class, students will automatically receive the Christian Basics Certificate (7 credits). This is the foundational certificate that opens up Christian Leaders Institute for further study by students.

2. Christian Leaders Certificate (23 credits)

After students complete the Christian Basics course, they are encouraged to work toward their Christian Leaders Certificate. This certificate covers the essential ministry training needed for many callings. The courses include:

Getting Started: Reproducible Walk with God and Christian Doctrine (7 credits)

Old Testament Survey (3 credits)

New Testament Survey (3 credits)

Church and Ministry (3 credits)

Pastoral Care and Marriage (3 credits)

Church History (4 credits)

Total Credits: 23

3. Commissioned Pastor Diploma (36 credits)

This ministry training diploma gives students the essentials they will need for leading their churches. The classes include:

Getting Started: Reproducible Walk with God and Christian Doctrine (7 credits)

Church History (4 credits)

Hermeneutics and Exegesis (3 credits)

Old Testament Survey (3 credits)

New Testament Survey (3 credits)

Preaching Methods (3 credits)

Pastoral Care and Marriage (3 credits)

Systematic Theology I (4 credits)

Systematic Theology II (3 credits)

Church and Ministry (3 credits)

Total Credits: 30

4. Ministry Diploma (42 Credit Hours)

The Diploma of Ministry is the first of our three advanced ministry training diplomas. This award says that students studied more areas of ministry training in-depth. This diploma will give them advanced knowledge in what they need to be a pastor, evangelist, ministry associate, church planter, chaplain, or other Christian leader. Some churches and denominations require this kind of a diploma for ordination.

Getting Started: Reproducible Walk with God and Christian Doctrine (7 credits)

Old Testament Survey (3 credits)

New Testament Survey (3 credits)

Hermeneutics and Exegesis (3 credits)

Church and Ministry (3 credits)

Pastoral Care and Marriage (3 credits)

Church History (4 credits)

Preaching Methods or Sermon Construction (3 credits)

Systematic Theology I (4 credits)

Systematic Theology II (3 credits)

Christian Ethics (3 credits)

Christian Apologetics (3 credits)

Total Credits: 45

5. Advanced Ministry Diploma (62 credits)

This Advanced Diploma of Ministry gives students knowledge and insight comparable to many seminaries. More in-depth knowledge of the various areas of study will serve them well in their ministry calling. Right now, Christian Leaders Institute is developing more thought-provoking courses.

Getting Started: Reproducible Walk with God and Christian Doctrine (7 credits)

Old Testament Survey (3 credits)

New Testament Survey (3 credits)

Hermeneutics and Exegesis (3 credits)

Church and Ministry (3 credits)

Pastoral Care and Marriage (3 credits)

Church History (4 credits)

Preaching Methods or Sermon Construction (3 credits)

Systematic Theology I (4 credits)

Systematic Theology II (3 credits)

Christian Ethics (3 credits)

Christian Apologetics (3 credits)

Total Credits: 62

6. Divinity Diploma (89 credits)

This Divinity Diploma is the highest award we grant to students at Christian Leaders Institute. This diploma digs deep into every area of study for ministry training. CLI eventually plans to offer this diploma with an "emphasis" as our class offering increases in the next few years, Lord willing.

Getting Started: Reproducible Walk with God and Christian Doctrine (7 credits)

Old Testament Survey (3 credits)

New Testament Survey (3 credits)

Hermeneutics and Exegesis (3 credits)

Church and Ministry (3 credits)

Pastoral Care and Marriage (3 Credits)

Church History (4 credits)

Preaching Methods or Sermon Construction (3 credits)

Systematic Theology I (4 credits)

Systematic Theology II (3 credits)

Christian Ethics (3 credits)

Christian Apologetics (3 credits)

Greek I (4 credits)

Greek II (4 credits)

Greek III (4 credits)

Total Credits: 89

7. Discipleship Diploma (30 credits)

This is another option that Christian Leaders Institute offers. After a student completes the foundational basics class, students can take any classes they want to accumulate 30 credits. This diploma is perfect for the Christian leader who wants to have a goal for continued studies. Many existing pastors may find this diploma very attractive.

Getting Started: Reproducible Walk with God and Christian Doctrine (7 credits)

Christian Leaders Institute classes (23 credits)

Total Credits: 30

John Knox the founder of the Presbyterian Church was a revival leader and had zeal for an alive and vibrant church. He had as much of the Holy Spirit passion of any revival leader that ever lived.

Knox prayed continually, "God, give me Scotland or I die!" Knox desperately prayed for seven years to God that Scotland would be revived back to God. God did bring revival to Scotland. And wherever Presbyterian Churches exist they are a testament to the revival that God brought about by John Knox.

But unlike Evan Roberts, John Knox believed in the importance of sound doctrine that must guide every ministry leader. Knox saw that many attacks would come to test leaders. Historically those who followed the true passion of John Knox believed in solid Biblical training and intense spiritual fervor. That is the type of leader that CLI is looking for. Someone who wants to be well grounded in scripture doctrine and who says,

"Give me Ghana or I die."

"Give me America or I die."

"Give me India or I die"

"Give me Turkey or I die"

Give me _____ or I die!

CHAPTER 7

BEING MENTORED REVIVAL LEADERS - EVERYONE NEEDS MENTORS

<u>Acts 4:36</u> Joseph, a Levite from Cyprus, whom the apostles called Barnabas (which means Son of Encouragement)

Dwight Moody brought revival to millions. By the time he died at age 62 he had preached to over 100,000 people. He started a Bible Institute, which has become a gold standard for teaching and mentoring effective pastors and evangelists. Moody Bible Institute has been an inspiration to Christian Leaders Institute.

Lyle Dorsett has written an excellent essay on Moody. In his essay, Dorset illustrated how necessary it was for Moody to have mentors. These mentors brought him to the faith and gave him the valuable training needed to give him a great start in his Christian walk. Dorset wrote,

> Dwight Moody's life in Christ began when he left the hardscrabble soil of northwestern Massachusetts. Leaving behind his grinding labor as a farm hand, the restless teen moved to Boston, where he found employment in an uncle's shoe store. Moody's godly

relative provided room, board, and a day job to his seventeen-year-old nephew with one condition: he must faithfully promise to attend Sunday school and church every week.

Young Moody kept his promise, and Uncle Lemuel Holton witnessed the answer to his prayers. Dwight heard the gospel story from his Sunday school teacher, Edward Kimball, who one Saturday stopped by Holton's shoe store where he found Dwight alone. Moody never forgot the day Kimball came behind the counter "and put his hand upon my shoulder, and talked to me about Christ and my soul. I had not felt I had a soul till then." Moody stood astounded by the presence of this man who had known him only a few weeks yet wept over his sins. Years later Moody said, "I don't remember what he said, but I can feel the power of that man's hand on my shoulder tonight." Within a few months, the young shoe store clerk surrendered his life to Christ and expressed a willingness to repent and be mentored in the faith by Edward Kimball and a few other men in Boston's Mount Vernon Congregational Church. The young convert admitted that he soon found himself in 'a conflict with my will. I had a terrible battle to surrender my will, and to take God's will.' http://www.cslewisinstitute.org/Profile_DL_Moody_Dorsett_Single-Page_Full_Article

Moody left the eastern United States and headed for Chicago, an emerging city on Lake Michigan in the Midwest of the USA. Moody had the gift of making money. He could have lost his spiritual focus, but he was willing to be mentored by another Christian leader. Her name was Mrs. H. Phillips. Dorset outlined this mentoring relationship as well,

> Despite his ambition to earn money, Moody purposively pursued his walk with the Lord. Soon after his arrival in Chicago, he began rooming and taking meals in the house of "Mother" H. Phillips. Mrs. Phillips not only housed and fed Moody, she held him accountable to pray and read his Bible daily and attend services at First Baptist, her home church. But Mother Phillips did more than mentor Moody; she encouraged him to assist her in city mission work. Thanks to the witness of this godly woman, Moody began an outreach to a growing throng of street children—thousands of impoverished boys and girls who roamed the streets and alleys of the neighborhoods where the lowest social and economic classes lived.
> http://www.cslewisinstitute.org/Profile_DL_Moody_Dorsett_Single-Page_Full_Article

Moody grew in his relationship with God as he continued to gain wealth in his business enterprises. There were leaders that invited Moody to Bible Studies and revival meetings in Chicago around 1857. Moody was called into bi-vocational ministry, like many who are studying at Christian Leaders Institute.

God brought another mentor into Moody's life. God led J. B. Stillson, a much older Christian Leader to serve as a spiritual mentor. Stillson taught Moody how to study the Bible. Soon he was using study aids including concordances and Bible dictionaries.

By the time the United States' Civil war broke out, Moody had received great amounts of mentorship and ministry training from well-grounded leaders and various sources. He became a chaplain for General Grant and tirelessly shared the Gospel and ministered to the dying. After the war he became an evangelist who led millions to Christ. He remembered the importance of the mentors in his life and set up Moody Bible Institute to be a mentoring place that continues as a ministry training school today.

What would have happened to Moody if God had not raised up these mentors?

Mentor's Call

What motivates a mentor? A mentor is motivated to help others advance, thus investing in the lives of others. Mentors are motivated to help others because they love to reproduce in others the various learning that they have received.

I remember asking Rich DeVos Sr. to be my mentor back in 1993. Rich loved the reproducing of Christianity. Based on what he learned in building Amway for a generation, he mentored me and introduced me to ideas, people, attitudes and challenges that helped build the culture that we both loved. He freely offered recognition when I accomplished something and invested in me to bring me to even greater ministry effectiveness.

Everyone Needs To Be In A Mentor Relationship

We expect Christian Leaders Institute students to welcome mentors into their lives. These mentors know the student or leader. If an existing pastor who is experienced comes into CLI for more training, we still encourage them to connect to a mentor that will help them to continue to grow and advance.

I have been a pastor since 1987, but I still need mentors. Christian Leaders Institute is entering into a new phase of existence. The founding phase is ending. Now we enter into creating an organization that will last a long time. I am going to need mentors to teach me what I do not know and support me in what I do know.

What Does A Christian Mentor Do?

Christian mentors are self-aware about their calling to build local Christian culture. In fact, they intuitively look for opportunities to help people fit in or make an impact. These mentors know that God is calling them to invest in the lives of potential difference makers. Barnabas was a mentor. If you look at him in relationship to Paul and Mark, you see that his calling was to mentor potential leaders. Let's look at Barnabas, the father of mentors.

I am going to list all the passages that mention the life and work of Barnabas; each of them illustrates how he was an early church mentor. From his life, we are going to come up with a portrait of a Biblical mentor.

1. Mentors Are Seen To Be Encouragers

    Mentors are recognized as leaders who notice those who need encouragement. Barnabas was seen that way. In fact, when he was first mentioned in the Bible by name in Acts 4:36, we see that the apostles had already changed his name from Joseph to Barnabas, which actually means Son of Encouragement:

    > Joseph, a Levite from Cyprus, whom the apostles called Barnabas (which means Son of Encouragement) (Acts 4:36)

    Something interesting to note is that they gave him standing in his title. Early church titles were very important. We have the title for Jesus, "Son of God". The title for Barnabas is Son of Encouragement. A mentor is recognized to be an encourager.

    If you are a student at CLI, we encourage you to find a mentor. I encourage you to find that Barnabas who is seen to be someone who will help you. Call your mentor, "Barnabas."

2. Mentors Are Generous With Resources

Mentors are not stingy. They take their resources of time and money and bring them to the feet of Jesus. Barnabas was generous with his resources. The second thing we read about him in the Bible is that he sold a field to help others in need:

> [Barnabas] sold a field he owned and brought the money and put it at the apostles' feet. (Acts 4:37)

Here was a guy who was already acknowledged for how he used his time to encourage others. Then on top of that he put his money where his mouth was. There was a need beyond what his encouragement brought. What did he do? Cashed in an asset to help.

This characteristic of a mentor is so important because the new potential leader needs that model of generosity. The church needs pastors who will be willing sponsors of another generation of pastors.

3. Mentors Will Make Connections

Mentors will introduce students into opportunities. They leverage who they know to help new leaders get opportunities for ministry. Barnabas did this to the point of taking a risk. We read in Acts 9 that Saul is blinded on the road to Damascus. He is called by God to be the chosen instrument to bring the gospel to the Gentiles. But Saul was known as the Christian persecutor who might be trying to play a trick on the church.

It was Barnabas who had the standing to make the introduction of Saul, later to be named Paul, to the apostles:

> When he came to Jerusalem, he tried to join the disciples, but they were all afraid of him, not believing that he really was a disciple. But Barnabas took him and brought him to the apostles. (Acts 9:26-27)

Let us be clear, a mentor does not just connect anyone and everyone. The disciple must have demonstrated that he/she is called and genuine. Barnabas saw in Saul the calling of God. It was this truth that compelled him to introduce Saul to the apostles.

Mentors see their role with those whom God has brought to them as an opportunity to connect potential leaders with opportunities for ministry. A mentor might help with ordination requirements at a local church or denomination. A mentor may help connect a student with a funding opportunity.

4. Mentors Are Promoters

Mentors speak well of those they are mentoring. Barnabas was one who spoke well of Saul. Barnabas saw in Saul his calling and character. I am sure he could have found a lot of negative to say about Saul. We all have that negative in us. Instead, Barnabas spoke well of the apostle and saw the positive:

> He told them how Saul on his journey had seen the Lord and that the Lord had spoken to him, and how in Damascus he had preached fearlessly in the name of Jesus. (Acts 9:27b)

Mentors appropriately and publicly build up the potential leader. Mentors talk that leader up. Mentors tell positive stories about potential leaders. These potential leaders do not threaten their mentors; their mentors want them to succeed.

5. Mentors Stay Connected In Ministry

Mentors follow the ministry training progress of students and, even after they graduate, they delight in their progress and partner with them in further ministry. Barnabas was mentoring Saul when he was being prepared, he introduced him to the apostles, and even later, Barnabas went looking for Saul and then partnered in ministry with Saul for a whole year. It was at this time that the followers of Jesus were first called Christians:

> So Barnabas went to Tarsus to look for Saul, and when he had found him, he brought him to Antioch. For a whole year they met with the church and taught a great many people. And in Antioch the disciples were first called Christians. (Acts 11:25-26)

Ministry capital is ultimately about leaders partnering together and building a culture that honors Christ. Those who have gone before the students, later work alongside those very students. Mentors really stay connected with their potential leaders even after they have finished the preparation stage and are ministering. Saul and Barnabas made such a team that the church at Antioch sent them on a mission together:

> While they were worshiping the Lord and fasting, the Holy Spirit said, "Set apart for me Barnabas and Saul for the work to which I have called them." (Acts 13:2)

6. Mentors Who become Less

There will be times when the one in training will be called to a special work by God. The mentored one will succeed beyond his mentor. Saul's name is changed to Paul and he is now the team leader. In Chapter 13 of Acts, Barnabas is still mentioned first, "the Holy Spirit said, "Set apart for me Barnabas and

Saul for the work to which I have called them." But Chapter 14 mentions Paul first:

> Paul and Barnabas appointed elders for them in each church and, with prayer and fasting, committed them to the Lord, in whom they had put their trust. (Acts 14:23)

Effective mentors are looking for people who will exceed them in impact. They will invest and encourage leaders to be their best for God. Paul and Barnabas were planting churches and appointing leaders together everywhere they went.

7. Mentors And Mentored Not Afraid Of Doing Their Own Thing

The relationship of the mentor and the mentored can change even as circumstances change. Paul and Barnabas parted company over a disagreement. I am so glad this stayed in the Bible. Sometimes a mentor and the one who is sponsored disagree about something. Barnabas and Paul disagreed about what to do with Mark to the extent that that they parted company.

Barnabas appeared to want to give Mark another opportunity to prove himself in ministry. Paul felt that it was risky to take someone who had buckled under pressure. When reading about their disagreement, I am impressed that they both went their own way and God's kingdom was advanced in their disagreement:

> Some time later Paul said to Barnabas, "Let us go back and visit the brothers in all the towns where we preached the word of the Lord and see how they are doing." Barnabas wanted to take John, also called Mark, with them, but Paul did not think it wise to take him, because he had deserted them in Pamphylia and had not continued with them in the work. They had such a sharp disagreement that they parted company. Barnabas took Mark and sailed for Cyprus, but Paul chose Silas and left, commended by the brothers to the grace of the Lord. (Acts 15:36-40)

Sometimes the mentor and the mentored one have disagreements, even sharp ones. I have seen a sponsored student sense the call to plant a new church. The sponsor disagrees. Eventually the mentor and the mentored one go their separate ways. At first they are uncomfortable about the split; however, after a while they see that the kingdom of God is advanced through it all.

At Christian Leaders Institute, a mentor is a huge asset for the student. When mentors give students opportunities to preach, lead and pray, the student greatly benefits.

More and more, Christian Leaders Institute will connect and build the connection between mentor and the mentored. Christian Leaders Institute will deliver high-quality Biblical ministry training, and mentors will do the finishing touches and provide a local context to the students. This will keep students blooming where they are planted.

Mentors Bring Ministry Opportunities

The mentors in a local people group are important in the training process. These mentors will help students interface with their local group. These mentors will make sure that there is a path of ordination for the students when they complete their training. The mentors will help students plug in and help them in their ordination at a local church or in a church-planting situation. CLI can bring excellent ministry training to the students; the mentor can bring excellent ministry opportunity to the students.

Most impactful Christian leaders of the past have benefited from excellent mentors. This is why we require that every new applicant to CLI put down a mentor because revival leaders have mentors. Where would Dwight Moody be without his mentors? Where would you be without your mentors?

CHAPTER 8

MENTORING REVIVAL LEADERS - EVERYONE IS A MENTOR

> 1 Thessalonians 5:11 Therefore encourage one another and build each other up, just as in fact you are doing.

Revival leaders inevitably reproduce more revival leaders. I saw the reproduction principle illustrated well by my mentor, Rich DeVos, Sr., the co-founder of the Amway Corporation. DeVos, a dedicated Christian, built a business with his partner Jay Van Andel whereby anyone could afford to build a business.

I remember in 1993 when Rich DeVos began to mentor me. I decided to join Amway as a business owner associate. I decided to join because I reasoned that if the co-founder of Amway was mentoring me, I should walk the path he helped create. My Amway experience was excellent.

I saw ordinary men and women do extraordinary things. People that you would not think could build a business, actually succeeded. I also saw that people who looked like they had the complete package to build a business, quit after a couple of weeks. I signed up over 80 new distributors in 6 months and really enjoyed the business. In fact, I had to figure out whether being an Amway distributor was my calling. After careful prayer and reflection, I renewed my resolve for ministry.

I learned much as an Amway distributor, by observing all these values up close and personal in Rich DeVos. He modeled and understood being a leader. I learned about so much that goes into building anything including a business, a church, and even an online Bible school. These things have helped me greatly in life and have laid the foundation for so much of what I have been called to pursue. I learned things like:

1. Get over the fear of meeting and talking to people while letting respect and love guide me.

    Treat everyone as an image bearer of God who is worth my time in that moment. People will see an elitist heart; they will sense if I only talk to them if I have a hidden agenda. I learned that God has a plan in every relationship He puts in my life.

2. Be a servant leader, not just an authority leader.

3. Leaders create platforms for others to do well.

    Jesus himself said to his disciples, "Anyone who wants to be first must be the very last, and the servant of all." (Mark 9:35). People sense if I have their best interest in mind or mine.

4. Work hard in a focused way.

    Hard work is a given. Focused hard work makes the most difference. For instance, sitting at the computer conducting research *about* selling is not actually selling.

5. Recruit everyone, but when you find leaders train them well.

    Leaders are the key to building anything sustainable. If you want to build a movement, look for leaders and give them the training they need to succeed.

6. Create a culture of reproducible knowledge, habits and sharing.

    If I wanted to build an Amway business, those I sponsored would need some knowledge of the products and the Amway culture. They would need to use the products habitually, and they would need to learn how to share what they used in their personal life. I sponsored an Egyptian neighbor who snuck into our kitchen while at our house and checked our cupboards to see if my wife and I used Amway products.

    This is so similar in Christianity. Christians get saved into a walk with God. They need knowledge of what Christianity actually is about. Someone needs to teach them who the God of the Bible is and how to walk with him. Someone needs to be able to communicate basic Bible teaching. Knowledge is very important.

Then there is the need to walk in daily habits. This walk with God is simple, involving talking and listening daily in their personal life, their marriage (if married), their family, their friends, their church and their connection to other Christians worldwide. They need to walk in a path of sharing their walk with God. This simple walk with God in Christ has been reproducible for 2000 years.

7. Recognize Achievements.

When someone does well, say so. Be real about this, but do not err on the stingy side of encouragement. I saw how important recognition was while doing an Amway business. This recognition would bring people to tears because they never thought anyone noticed what they did.

Many times, Christians do not encourage or compliment those who are faithful in building up the church because we do not want pride to characterize our churches. But the Bible does teach that we ought to recognize those who live according to the pattern that was given. Philippians 3:17 says, "Join with others in following my example, brothers, and take note of those who live according to the pattern we gave you."

8. See the potential in people without prequalifying them.

Rich DeVos sure practiced what he preached. From day one in our mentoring relationship, Rich saw the potential in me despite the fact that I had and still have such a long way to go. The Amway organization teaches this as a core value. So many of their leaders are now leaders because someone gave them an opportunity to start a business with almost no start-up capital. Successful Amway associates were a delight to be around because they were often intrinsically motivated to do the business out of passion and calling and not out of the force of debt.

At Christian Leaders Institute, we are trying to allow leaders and potential leaders to get their ministry training to become a pastor at little cost, so that everyone who is called gets an opportunity. This is such a core value that we have learned to keep operating expenses so low that everyone who finishes the getting started class gets free tuition.

We do ask students to donate to help other students get the training. We find that the students that finish the getting started class are intrinsically motivated to do their studies. A large investment of money or relocation is not the force that motivates them to complete their studies. They complete their training because they know they need it. Plus, the low cost to each student allows students from the poorest of poor countries and students from anywhere to get training no matter what their situation is.

9. Use technology to serve your purpose.

I always loved this about Amway. In the early 1990s, when I was involved with Amway, they were always at the cutting edge of using technology to help their leaders do better. Today, I understand that much of the business is driven by effective use of the Internet.

As we talked about earlier in this book, the conversion box of the Internet was invented and became a powerful tool now spreading to bring high quality ministry training everywhere.

10. Build where you are and with the people with whom you live.

   Rich would encourage me to help people bloom where they were planted. The Amway leaders would help each person write down on a piece of paper everyone they knew, so that they could contact each of them to promote their products. Some people did not like this, but this is really where the leaders are discovered. If leaders will share their passion and products with those they know, they will be more likely to share their passion and their products with people they do not know.

   Christian Leaders Institute is all about having leaders bloom where they are planted. We bring the training to students' homes, to their context with their sponsors. We believe that there already exists relational capital that can be built on for the gospel of Jesus Christ and the building and the strengthening of the Church.

I am so happy and feel so blessed by the mentorship of Rich DeVos, one of the founding board members of Christian Leaders Institute. As I look at what Amway has done from an eagle's point of view, it is very much similar to the topic of this book. Amway was about planting a culture of entrepreneurship, a culture where anyone can be a business owner.

This culture is not just about selling books and tapes about how to build businesses; this is a culture where there are actually products and services used by real people. This culture builds to where now Amway is worldwide and there are products and services available everywhere, but more importantly, there are business owners who are leaders in their cultures. The leaders bloom where they are planted. They start reaching people who reach even more people. This culture keeps spreading and includes more and more leaders every day.

From the eagle's point of view, I noticed that every successful Amway distributor was a product user themselves. Further, they too were mentoring others like they were mentored. This meant that they committed to a product-use lifestyle and they trained, and boldly mentored, others into that lifestyle. Some of the most fearless people I have ever seen were Amway business owners. I always admired that boldness. I also noticed that these distributors got into the habit of helping people even when it had nothing to do with Amway. They mentored people into a better life, whatever that would mean in that local context.

Everyone is A Sponsor

My involvement with Amway illustrated something that was just plain true. Mentors make a culture grow. And whether a formal system like Amway, where every relationship is kept track of, or in informal relationships, leaders step forward to create culture. Mentors make things happen. Mentors really are the leaders of a society. I have noticed that most people have a few topics where they would be considered "mentors." Just get someone talking about what interests them and you will find that they willingly lead others in their pursuits. If I may put it metaphorically, everyone is building something. I developed a deep interest in having Rich DeVos mentor me in 1993 because I had seen an enthusiastic Amway distributor attempt to get me to join Amway. This distributor truly impressed me.

I concluded that we needed that kind of enthusiasm in Christians sponsoring their neighbors into a walk with God. I realize that we do not want to be annoying or too pushy, but who can fault us for our passion, love and concern for our fellow humans. If Christianity is true, and we believe it to be, we can't just sit back and say, "Whatever." We really need to participate in sponsoring this eternal salvation culture to spread through the entire earth.

So while we enjoy many passions and activities on this earth, we need to realize that each of us also is a sponsor in building Christianity. In Christianity, we can take on different types of sponsoring roles, but we are still nonetheless called to build with our time, talents and resources.

Ministry Opportunities

On the ministry side, we give students,, in whatever their situation, the opportunity to go as far as they want to go. In the year 2012-2013 this means that over 20,000 new applications were taken and these students were given an account to be a student at Christian Leaders Institute. They were given their "kit," called the Getting Started Class; that kit was free. All they had to invest was their time and an Internet connection. Of those over 20,000 new students, over 2,000 of them completed the Getting Started Class and went deeper into their ministry training. These students were plugged in with their local mentor/sponsor. A growing number of students from all over the world are now even donating money to sponsor others in gaining quality ministry training.

Encouragement Opportunities

On the encouragement side, we started an encouragement program for Christians who wanted to become, like Barnabas, a son or daughter of encouragement. We give mature believers an opportunity to bring a mission trip right into their homes or businesses. If your calling is to connect with, pray for and encourage ministry students to finish their preparations, we want to partner with you and give you the encouragement "kit" to prepare you to be an encourager at CLI.

This encouragement program is for pastors, former students, mature Christians, and donors to Christian Leaders Institute. This program takes encouragers on a "Barnabas trip."

Encouragers take a "getting started class" and are taught how to directly talk to current students and encourage them in their calling.

If you are reading this book and desire to encourage our students, go to www.christianleaders.net to find out more information.

Donation Opportunities

On the donation side, we are giving opportunities for the Christian community to make an investment in the preparation of called Christian leaders.

We respect the fact that every Christian donor has a calling to build the kingdom of God. Our goal is to serve their dream. When donors give gifts to CLI, we think of it as directly and efficiently sponsoring ministry globally. We want to help Christians sponsor as much building of Christian ministry capital as possible.

CHAPTER 9

GROUPING REVIVAL LEADERS – MENTOR CENTERS LOCALLY AND WORLDWIDE

Romans 15:14 I myself am convinced, my brothers, that you yourselves are full of goodness, complete in knowledge and competent to instruct one another.

Imagine being born a slave in the seventeen hundreds in Delaware, USA. Your family was sold to another owner. That owner comes on financial hard times and sells your mother and some of your siblings. Imagine also the gospel entering into your life. It has changed you. But the same gospel that has taken the bitterness of slavery away from you has also changed your owner. Your owner allows you to buy yourself out of slavery. You are set free to a world of great changes. The United States of America is being founded and freedom from tyranny is in the air.

What would you do with your freedom? The country is poor. You are poor. But you are called to proclaim the gospel.

Richard Allen, a newly freed slave, found himself called to be trained for ministry. He could not afford to go to a college or a seminary. He could barely feed himself. He was looking to find where God wanted him.

At that same time, the newly forming Methodist movement was spreading in the young nation. These leaders created mentor relationships where called lay leaders would study to prepare themselves for bi-vocational ministry service. One of these leaders was named Francis Asbury who was mentored and appointed by John Wesley, the founder of the Methodist movement. Asbury created places that mentored bi-vocational leaders to spread the gospel as pastors, church planters and missionaries to bring people back to God. Asbury created a place for called leaders to be trained for ministry.

Richard S. Newman wrote in his biography of Richard Allen,

This is where Richard Allen found himself in 1790. The church also actively recruited blacks like Allen, offering them organizational duties as exhorters and preachers. In the upper Chesapeake, Francis Asbury relied on Allen to spread the gospel to people of color. But he was not the only black preacher to gain notoriety during the Revolutionary era. His generation included a half-dozen major black ministers, many of whom had Methodist connections: John Jea, Absalom Jones, Boston King, John Marrant, George White, and Peter Williams. For them, as for Allen, the light of revelation was powerful enough to destroy the shackles of slavery. Richard S. Newman (2008-03-01). Freedom's Prophet (Kindle Locations 900-904). NYU Press. Kindle Edition.

In this mentoring place with the founding leaders of the America Methodist movement, Richard Allen was preparing for ministry service. He met for regular encouragement. Each leader in this mentor center had mentors. The mentors had mentors. These were lifelong ministry relationships.

Newman writes about how Asbury and Allen stayed close even as their duties expanded in different directions.

In 1803, Allen celebrated their two decades of fellowship by purchasing a horse for Asbury (for the not-unsubstantial sum of ninety dollars). That token of gratitude, gladly accepted by Asbury (who had worn out his own mare), was but a small repayment for Asbury's longtime assistance to Allen. When Allen broke from white Methodists at St. George's in the early 1790s, Asbury gave the inaugural address to the new black church. It was Asbury too who ordained Allen as the first black Methodist deacon in 1799. And of course, in 1785, only a bit removed from slavery and just beginning his own itinerancy, Allen received his first major boost from Asbury, who had actually called for the talented young exhorter by name. Come and help me save souls, he asked Allen. Here, Allen recalled, was a bishop who not only recalled a black man's full name but wanted his help. Richard S. Newman (2008-03-01). Freedom's Prophet (Kindle Locations 1026-1034). NYU Press. Kindle Edition.

A Culture of Mentorship

Francis Asbury, that great Methodist leader, recruited men like bi-vocational Richard Allen and many others in his mentor center. When they were new into ministry, he provided them with the intellectual training needed. When they were looking for ministry opportunities, he guided them and promoted them to fulfill their calling and make the greatest possible impact. The story of Richard Allen is notable for many reasons. Here a freed slave starts the largest African American denomination. The World Council of Churches estimates the membership of the AME Church at around 2,500,000, with 3817 pastors, 21 bishops and 7000 congregations.

I want to reproduce the dynamics that reproduce Christian Leaders like Richard Allen. The early Methodists like John Wesley and Francis Asbury were brilliant in creating mentor centers, which created a very powerful movement of revival. These leaders created a culture of mentorship, which produced many revival leaders who became circuit riders for the spread of revival.

The Mentorship Driven Ministry Training

Christian Leaders Institute positions its online ministry training in the culture of mentorship. This mentorship could be right where a new student is in a mentor relationship with a pastor. This mentorship could include the pastor and some new local recruits that will meet in a mentor center at the local church or other location. This mentorship could occur in a denominationally sponsored mentor center in a specific geographic location.

The Mentor Center Concept

Over the past 7 years, Christian Leaders Institute has labored online to strengthen the faith of any Christian with a ministry dream. We have sought to make this ministry training mentor supported.

Now CLI will begin resourcing indigenous Ministry Mentor Centers, where local Christian leaders and churches will be able to offer local gathering points. These geographic touch-points will make the campus of Christian Leaders Institute physically spread throughout the world.

Imagine the strength of the universal church if ANY local church with Internet access could deliver advanced ministry training straight to their congregants. We are calling these new touch-points: Ministry Mentor Centers.

The New Paradigm Shift

Bible schools and seminaries have typically been geographically locked down to one location, with maybe a few satellite campuses. These rare locations forced students to relocate to one of these areas if they wanted training. Then, after gleaning as much as they could, students would often once again relocate to a church in some other area.

The coming of the Internet has brought changes to how ministry training is delivered. Many Bible schools like Liberty University along with many seminaries such as Calvin Seminary now offer online classes through distance learning programs. The epicenter of the training is still the professors at the home base institute. Often accreditation models require this.

Christian Leaders Institute is about to launch a new initiative that completely changes the epicenter of ministry training.

Christian Leaders Institute plans to launch Ministry Mentor Centers. These ministry mentor centers will eventually become hundreds of epicenters of ministry training.

How Ministry Mentor Centers Work

CLI will offer their entire curriculum of ministry training classes, lectures and quizzes to local ministry mentor centers spread throughout the world. These ministry mentor centers will bring students together in a local geographic place recruited by local leaders and CLI's efforts. These local places will be the campuses of CLI that support local mentors in their efforts to train new pastors and leaders.

In the end, CLI will not only continue to offer world class online ministry training, CLI will also begin planting local Bible schools and seminaries, which we call Ministry Mentor Centers. Corporate CLI beams the content to support local leaders in their efforts to train new leaders for revival.

Mentor Centers

Existing Leader Mentor Centers: Because Christian Leaders Institute positions its training to be utilized by local leaders, new possibilities are open for creating a mentor culture that cultivates revival leaders for your church or your community. Existing leaders are invited to enroll at Christian Leaders Institute and take the Getting Started Class. This class will give existing leaders a good understanding of the online ministry training that they will share with their recruits. Even existing pastors who have advanced training need to take this one class to start a mentor center. Christian Leaders

Institute does allow existing leaders to take the class at the same time their recruits are taking it. Students who complete certificates or diplomas will download that certificate or diploma and have it given to them officially at the mentor center.

Peer Mentor Centers: An active student at CLI could also start a peer mentor center if they have completed the getting started class and they have support from their local pastor or mentor leader. This peer sponsored mentor center holds students accountable in a "study group" setting. Each student may have their own individual mentors who help them process their ministry training. When students finish diplomas, those diplomas are downloaded by the student to be given to them by their individual mentor or pastor.

Seminary Sponsored Mentor Centers: Seminaries who have to face budget cuts or limited resources may desire to partner with Christian Leaders Institute to create a partnership location whereby Christian Leaders Institute provides the lectures, ministry training content, and study accountability such as quizzes. CLI will also keep track of all grades and grant diplomas, which can be downloaded by the student and given at the seminary sponsored mentor center location.

Market Place Sponsored Mentor Centers: Christian civic or business leaders or organizations may want to offer mentor centers. These centers could meet at lunch hour or after work. Imagine Businesses or Civic organizations starting ministry training.

Christian School Sponsored Mentor Centers: Christian high schools or colleges may want to sponsor local mentor centers to cover certain areas of their curriculum and also provide a place for the training of young people for ministry. Christian Leaders Institute will provide the lectures, ministry training content, and study accountability such as quizzes. CLI will also keep track of all grades and grant diplomas, which can be downloaded by the student and given at the school/college sponsored mentor center location.

Ministry Sponsored Mentor Centers: Ministries that do local or international work may consider starting a mentor center using the resources of Christian Leaders Institute. CLI has excellent accountability and can provide your donors with excellent reports. We would consider partnering with qualified ministries. Contact CLI for more details.

Mission Committee or Church Sponsored Mentor Centers: A local church may have vision for indigenous leader training in a specific geographic area. Churches can partner with Christian Leaders Institute to start or support a mentor center in another location other than their church. This mentor center could be any of those already listed. Christian Leaders Institute may help co-ordinate the reports of the mentor center project.

Individual Donor Sponsored Mentor Centers: Individuals or couples may sense the call to donate to support indigenous leaders in mentoring and educating revival leaders. This mentor center could be any of those already listed. Christian Leaders Institute may help co-ordinate the reports of the mentor center project.

Creating Revival Leader Cultivation Culture

I was wondering if there is a mentor center model in the Bible. I can think of Jesus and his disciples. That was a mentor center that included Jesus, our Lord. He spent time teaching, mentoring and preparing his disciples for bringing all nations back to God.

I see in the book of Acts how these disciples brought the gospel to the ends of the earth.

I love reading Romans 16, and I actually read Romans 16 often. It is truly one of my favorite Bible passages. I have even memorized portions of Romans 16. I have often imagined and dreamed about how leaders can start new movements that in thirty years would create a culture of vital Christianity spreading like it did in the early church.

I believe that the mentor centers have that kind of potential. I can imagine the Apostle Paul writing Romans 16. He has spent years mentoring new leaders. He has created mentor centers in various places in the Roman world. The lines between church and mentor centers were blurred in many places. Each church planted was very committed to cultivate leaders. New converts did not just sit in their pews, they were expected to learn, grow, and reach their neighbors based on the gift given.

In Romans 16, I see one of the apostle Paul's most gratifying moments. Read this in light of what you have read about mentor centers. Pretend that you are the apostle Paul and you have spent your life mentoring leaders and creating mentor centers where leaders are being developed and churches are being planted. You, like the apostle Paul, may be able to write a letter like this someday to those you have participated in raising up as leaders for revival. I have taken the verse break out so you can just absorb the leader culture that the Apostle Paul had created by setting up his era versions of mentor centers.

Romans 16:1-27 (Mentor Center Culture)

I commend to you our sister Phoebe, a servant of the church in Cenchrea. I ask you to receive her in the Lord in a way worthy of the saints and to give her any help she may need from you, for she has been a great help to many people, including me.

Greet Priscilla and Aquila, my fellow workers in Christ Jesus. They risked their lives for me. Not only I but all the churches of the Gentiles are grateful to them. Greet also the church that meets at their house.

Greet my dear friend Epenetus, who was the first convert to Christ in the province of Asia.

Greet Mary, who worked very hard for you.

Greet Andronicus and Junias, my relatives who have been in prison with me. They are outstanding among the apostles, and they were in Christ before I was.

Greet Ampliatus, whom I love in the Lord.

Greet Urbanus, our fellow worker in Christ, and my dear friend Stachys.
Greet Apelles, tested and approved in Christ.

Greet those who belong to the household of Aristobulus.

Greet Herodion, my relative.

Greet those in the household of Narcissus who are in the Lord.

Greet Tryphena and Tryphosa, those women who work hard in the Lord.

Greet my dear friend Persis, another woman who has worked very hard in the Lord.

Greet Rufus, chosen in the Lord, and his mother, who has been a mother to me, too.

Greet Asyncritus, Phlegon, Hermes, Patrobas, Hermas and the brothers with them.

Greet Philologus, Julia, Nereus and his sister, and Olympas and all the saints with them.

Greet one another with a holy kiss. All the churches of Christ send greetings.

I urge you, brothers, to watch out for those who cause divisions and put obstacles in your way that are contrary to the teaching you have learned. Keep away from them. For such people are not serving our Lord Christ, but their own appetites. By smooth talk and flattery they deceive the minds of naive people.

Everyone has heard about your obedience, so I am full of joy over you; but I want you to be wise about what is good, and innocent about what is evil.

The God of peace will soon crush Satan under your feet.

The grace of our Lord Jesus be with you.

Timothy, my fellow worker, sends his greetings to you, as do Lucius, Jason and Sosipater, my relatives.

I, Tertius, who wrote down this letter, greet you in the Lord.

Gaius, whose hospitality I and the whole church here enjoy, sends you his greetings.

Erastus, who is the city's director of public works, and our brother Quartus send you their greetings.

Now to him who is able to establish you by my gospel and the proclamation of Jesus Christ, according to the revelation of the mystery hidden for long ages past, but now revealed and made known through the prophetic writings by the command of the eternal God, so that all nations might believe and obey him— to the only wise God be glory forever through Jesus Christ! Amen.
Now to him who is able to establish you in accordance with my gospel, the message I proclaim about Jesus Christ, in keeping with the revelation of the mystery hidden for long

ages past, but now revealed and made known through the prophetic writings by the command of the eternal God, so that all the Gentiles might come to faith and obedience—to the only wise God be glory forever through Jesus Christ! Amen.

Impressive. This was not just a church in Rome. This is a mentor center where leaders are being cultivated and readied for more reaching of people to come back to God.

I began this chapter talking about Richard Allen and Francis Asbury. From that mentor relationship spawned more mentor relationships, which became mentor centers, which became churches. This method of raising up leaders has worked and I want to see this method cultivated more and more in every place on earth.

Imagine what Richard Allen could have written in his "Romans 16" letter.

Conclusion

There are many ways to get involved at Christian Leaders Institute. God may be calling you to bring revival using the resources at CLI.

Training

If you are sensing the call into ministry, CLI will give you the opportunity to explore that calling and receive training free of charge. Apply at www.christianleadersinstitute.org

Mentor Centers

There are many types of mentor centers you can start. Chapter nine talks about the mentor center concept. Email hreyenga@christianleaders.net if you are interested in starting a mentor center.

Giving

As you pray and think about where you will invest your resources, I ask that you will consider these reasons for sponsoring ministry leaders at Christian Leaders Institute.

1. Build on the missions movement of the past, training the children of that movement. The Internet is increasingly available even in the remotest parts of the world. Christian Leaders Institute will bring your sponsorship there.

2. Efficiently invest your mission capital to make a large impact. Christian Leaders Institute is very efficient in leveraging your resources. A typical seminary needs from $10,000 to $40,000 per student per year to deliver high-quality ministry training. Christian Leaders Institute has got this training cost down to less than $300 dollars per year per Christian Basics graduate and above.
3. Courses are designed to be completely web Indigenous, updated, improved, and used again and again. We put up courses from academically trained and ministry tested professors who hold higher degrees. We video these professors and use the course materials again and again.
4. Our content can come from previously recorded video content, including deceased leaders like Dr. Francis Schaeffer or retired leaders like Dr. Edwin Roels, and in partnership with organizations like Vision Video and Christian History. We are now partnering with Ray Vander Laan in a partnership that includes Focus on the Family, The Way of the Shepard, and The Prince Foundation. We will integrate

5. Ray Vander Laan's material and use it where it will make great impact.
   5. Our fundraising ratios have historically been very low with administration and fundraising below 5 percent of the budget. We plan to keep this as low as possible. We are hoping to keep that percentage below 20 percent of the budget.

Jennifer Santo wanted us to let her thank you for what this training means to her.

> "Hello generous donors. I am greatly appreciative of those of you that donate to Christian Leaders Institute. With this help, I will be able to achieve the goals Christ has set out for my life. I want to help those outside that have felt like they have no hope to live for. My father used to be a severe drug addict and alcoholic. I grew up in that environment believing that was normal, but when I gave my life to Christ I realized there was an even deeper issue. My dad needed God's love more than ever because he was headed down a life of total ruin.

"I want to help people like my dad. I want those types of people to be able to have a second chance at life, to be able to know that there are 'more reasons to live than to die.' I've always wanted to go to a Bible institute, but could not afford it. With this opportunity to have a free scholarship, it means the world to me to be able to enhance my knowledge of God's perfect word. God is good. I came to Christ in October 2006. That was when I met the love of my life, my boyfriend. He has helped me so much and he was the one that took me to his church where I am now a member.

"I am not involved in ministry right now, but that is why I joined Christian Leaders Institute. I feel God's calling on my life right now, and I am responding to this calling. I pray God expands my wisdom of His word and continues to show me to believe in Him and believe in myself. I do not want to underestimate myself, but I want to believe that the power invested in me has been given to me by God. Just as he did for Moses, Paul, and even Jesus, God can do for me."

Donate online at https://www.christianleadersinstitute.org/donate.html

Let's build and strengthen the church together, as students, encouragers and donors, so that the gospel continues to reach and transform this world.

2 Corinthians 4:15 "All this is for your benefit, so that the grace that is reaching more and more people may cause thanksgiving to overflow to the glory of God."

Volunteering to Start and Build Encourager Groups

Christian Leaders Institute is seeking to recruit revival encouragement leaders. Groups can meet in many places like homes, churches, or businesses. These groups can meet weekly, bi-monthly or even monthly.

Agenda of the Monthly Meeting:

1. Devotions
2. Chat with a student live to lift in prayer or read a profile of a CLI student found at the CLI website. Start a prayer list with this person or persons.
3. Pray for any local revival needs.

4. Pray for worldwide revival, including the work of CLI volunteer positions.
5. Optional: Take an offering for CLI's work.

Revival Encourager Group – How to Start one?

Maybe you or someone you know is called to be a recruiter of encouragers who will meet in your local area. A recruiter will:

1. Sign up as an encourager at CLI. There is a basic class the encourager will take. Go to www.christianleaders.net

2. Invite people to join the local *Encouragement Group.*

3. Follow the simple agenda of the meeting.

4. Recruit other recruiters who will set up more encouragement groups.

5. Email hreyenga@christianleaders.net if you are interested in starting a group or in becoming a recruiter in a local church, in a region, or in a denomination.

I end this book with a quote from a student from China. This quote is taken from our "Mission and Revival" class, the final paper. I am humbled that CLI gets to train this leader as a future revival leader in China.

> Yes, we need revival. But revival comes with a price. That's the price I'm willing to pay after taking this course. I'm willing to live a life of humility because God cannot use the proud. He instead resists the proud (James 4:6; 1 Peter 5:5).

I'm willing by the grace of God to build a prayer altar to seek the face of God on a regular basis specifically for a revival where I am. I am willing to turn away and run away... in fact flee from anything anti-God.

I believe that because God has not changed; because God is not man that He should lie; because God is faithful to His Word; because God is no respecter of persons; He will pour out His revival on all who decide to seek His face for revival.

"Thank you CLI for this training which is stirring and firing my spirit to pray until revival comes. God has used one man before. God can use me! God can use anyone!."

Lord, Revive us again!

Make a Donation for Training Revival Leaders:

Information (please print) or visit https://www.christianleadersinstitute.org/donate.html (Tear this out)

Name _____

Address _____

City, ST Zip Code _____

Phone: _____

Email _____

I (we) plan to make this contribution in the form of: ☐cash ☐check ☐credit card ☐other.

Credit card type | Exp. date _____

Credit card number _____

Authorized signature _____

Please make checks, or other gifts payable to: Christian Leaders Institute
614 Fulton Street,
Grand Haven, MI 49417

ABOUT THE AUTHOR

Henry Reyenga Jr. has planted four new churches and has replanted one in the United States of America. He has worked for the international ministry of the Bible League for four years. He has been a pastor since 1988. In 2002, Henry founded Christian Leaders Institute which started offering Internet classes in 2006 with six new students. In 2012-2013, over 25,000 new students enrolled at Christian Leaders Institute, with over 2,500 active students.

Henry Reyenga is married to Pam Reyenga, they five children and nine grandchildren.

Made in the USA
Charleston, SC
24 June 2014